W9-ACK-289

Shakespeare
Explained

Macbeth

RICHARD ANDERSEN

INTRODUCTION BY JOSEPH SOBRAN

Marshall Cavendish
Benchmark
New York

FOR MY STUDENTS, WITH AFFECTION AND
APPRECIATION FOR ALL THEY'VE TAUGHT ME

Series consultant: Richard Larkin

Marshall Cavendish
99 White Plains Road
Tarrytown, New York 10591
www.marshallcavendish.us

Library of Congress Cataloging-in-Publication Data
Andersen, Richard, 1946-
Macbeth / by Richard Andersen.
p. cm. — (Shakespeare explained)
Includes bibliographical references and index.
Summary: "A literary analysis of the play Macbeth. Includes information on
the history and culture of Elizabethan England"—Provided by publisher.
ISBN 978-0-7614-3029-2 (alk. paper)
1. Shakespeare, William, 1564-1616. Macbeth—Juvenile literature. I. Title.
PR2823.A925 2009
822.3'3—dc22
2008014408

Photo research by: Linda Sykes

David Fisher, Oxford, UK: front cover; Michael Caven/istockphoto: back cover, 8, 25;
iStockphoto: 1; Neven Mendrila/Shutterstock: 3; Raciro/iStockphoto: 4; Art Parts RF: 6, 13, 24, 32;
©Nik Wheeler/Corbis: 11; Portraitgalerie, Schloss Ambras, Inssbruck, Austria/Erich Lessing/Art
Resource, NY: 18; AA World Travel Library/Alamy: 20; ©Hideo Kurihara/Alamy: 22; © Corbis
Sygma: 27; ©Andrew Fox/ Corbis: 30; Royal Shakespeare Collection: 37, 44, 63, 67; The Everett
Collection: 41; Getty Images: 47; The Granger Collection: 51, 93; Ruth Fremson/*The New York
Times*/Redux: 56; Columbia/The Kobal Collection: 77; ©Arclight Films/The Everett Collection: 87.

Editor: Deborah Grahame
Publisher: Michelle Bisson
Art Director: Anahid Hamparian
Series Design: Kay Petronio

Printed in Malaysia
135642

Contents

Shakespeare and His World

WILLIAM SHAKESPEARE, OFTEN NICKNAMED "THE BARD," IS, BEYOND ANY COMPARISON, THE MOST TOWERING NAME IN ENGLISH LITERATURE. MANY CONSIDER HIS PLAYS THE GREATEST EVER WRITTEN. HE STANDS OUT EVEN AMONG GENIUSES.

Yet the Bard is also closer to our hearts than lesser writers, and his tremendous reputation should neither intimidate us nor prevent us from enjoying the simple delights he offers in such abundance. It is as if he had written for each of us personally. As he himself put it, "One touch of nature makes the whole world kin."

Such tragedies as *Hamlet*, *Romeo and Juliet*, and *Macbeth* are world-famous, still performed on stage and in films. These and others have also been adapted for radio, television, opera, ballet, pantomime, novels, comic books, and other media. Two of the best ways to become familiar with them are to watch some of the many fine movies that have been made of them and to listen to recordings of them by some of the world's great actors.

Even Shakespeare's individual characters have a life of their own, like real historical figures. Hamlet is still regarded as the most challenging role ever written for an actor. Roughly as many whole books have been written about Hamlet, an imaginary character, as about actual historical figures such as Abraham Lincoln and Napoleon Bonaparte.

Shakespeare created an amazing variety of vivid characters. One of Shakespeare's most peculiar traits was that he loved his characters so much—even some of his villains and secondary or comic characters— that at times he let them run away with the play, stealing attention from his heroes and heroines.

So in *A Midsummer Night's Dream* audiences remember the absurd and lovable fool Bottom the Weaver better than the lovers who are the main characters. Romeo's friend Mercutio is more fiery and witty than Romeo himself; legend claims that Shakespeare said he had to kill Mercutio or Mercutio would have killed the play.

Shakespeare also wrote dozens of comedies and historical plays, as well as nondramatic poems. Although his tragedies are now regarded as his greatest works, he freely mixed them with comedy and history. And his sonnets are among the supreme love poems in the English language.

It is Shakespeare's mastery of the English language that keeps his words familiar to us today. Every literate person knows dramatic lines such as "Wherefore art thou Romeo?"; "My kingdom for a horse!"; "To be or not to be: that is the question"; "Friends, Romans, countrymen, lend me your ears"; and "What fools these mortals be!" Shakespeare's sonnets are noted for their sweetness: "Shall I compare thee to a summer's day?"

FAIR IS FOUL AND FOUL IS FAIR

SHAKESPEARE'S LANGUAGE

WITHOUT A DOUBT, SHAKESPEARE WAS THE GREATEST MASTER OF THE ENGLISH LANGUAGE WHO EVER LIVED. BUT JUST WHAT DOES THAT MEAN?

Shakespeare's vocabulary was huge, full of references to the Bible as well as Greek and Roman mythology. Yet his most brilliant phrases often combine very simple and familiar words:

"WHAT'S IN A NAME? THAT WHICH WE CALL A ROSE BY ANY OTHER NAME WOULD SMELL AS SWEET."

He has delighted countless millions of readers. And we know him only through his language. He has shaped modern English far more than any other writer.

Or, to put it in more personal terms, you probably quote his words several times every day without realizing it, even if you have never suspected that Shakespeare could be a source of pleasure to you.

So why do so many English-speaking readers find his language so difficult? It is our language, too, but it has changed so much that it is no longer quite the same language—nor a completely different one, either.

Shakespeare's English and ours overlap without being identical. He would have some difficulty understanding us, too! Many of our everyday words and phrases would baffle him.

Shakespeare, for example, would not know what we meant by a *car,* a *radio,* a *movie,* a *television,* a *computer,* or a *sitcom,* since these things did not even exist in his time. Our old-fashioned term *railroad train,* would be unimaginable to him, far in the distant future. We would have to explain to him (if we could) what *nuclear weapons, electricity,* and *democracy* are. He would also be a little puzzled by common expressions such as *high-tech, feel the heat, approval ratings, war criminal, judgmental,* and *whoopie cushion.*

So how can we call him "the greatest master of the English language"? It might seem as if he barely spoke English at all! (He would, however, recognize much of our dirty slang, even if he pronounced it slightly differently. His plays also contain many racial insults to Jews, Africans, Italians, Irish, and others. Today he would be called "insensitive.")

Many of the words of Shakespeare's time have become archaic. Words like *thou, thee, thy, thyself,* and *thine,* which were among the most common words in the language in Shakespeare's day, have all but disappeared today. We simply say *you* for both singular and plural, formal and familiar. Most other modern languages have kept their *thou.*

Sometimes the same words now have different meanings. We are apt to be misled by such simple, familiar words as *kind, wonderful, waste, just,* and *dear,* which he often uses in ways that differ from our usage.

Shakespeare also doesn't always use the words we expect to hear, the words that we ourselves would naturally use. When we might automatically say, "I beg your pardon" or just "Sorry," he might say, "I cry you mercy."

Often a glossary and footnotes will solve all three of these problems for us. But it is most important to bear in mind that Shakespeare was often hard for his first audiences to understand. Even in his own time his rich language was challenging. And this was deliberate. Shakespeare was inventing his own kind of English. It remains unique today.

A child doesn't learn to talk by using a dictionary. Children learn first by sheer immersion. We teach babies by pointing at things and saying their names. Yet the toddler always learns faster than we can teach! Even as babies we are geniuses. Dictionaries can help us later, when we already speak and read the language well (and learn more slowly).

So the best way to learn Shakespeare is not to depend on the footnotes and glossary too much, but instead to be like a baby: just get into the flow of the language. Go to performances of the plays or watch movies of them.

THE LANGUAGE HAS A MAGICAL WAY OF TEACHING ITSELF, IF WE LET IT. THERE IS NO REASON TO FEEL STUPID OR FRUSTRATED WHEN IT DOESN'T COME EASILY.

Hundreds of phrases have entered the English language from *Hamlet* alone, including "to hold, as t'were, the mirror up to nature"; "murder most foul"; "the thousand natural shocks that flesh is heir to"; "flaming youth"; "a countenance more in sorrow than in anger"; "the play's the thing"; "neither a borrower nor a lender be"; "in my mind's eye"; "something is rotten in the state of Denmark"; "alas, poor Yorick"; and "the lady doth protest too much, methinks."

From other plays we get the phrases "star-crossed lovers"; "what's in a name?"; "we have scotched the snake, not killed it"; "one fell swoop"; "it was Greek to me;" "I come to bury Caesar, not to praise him"; and "the most unkindest cut of all"—all these are among our household words. In fact, Shakespeare even gave us the expression "household words." No wonder his contemporaries marveled at his "fine filed phrase" and swooned at the "mellifluous and honey-tongued Shakespeare."

Shakespeare's words seem to combine music, magic, wisdom, and humor:

"THE COURSE OF TRUE LOVE NEVER DID RUN SMOOTH."

"HE JESTS AT SCARS THAT NEVER FELT A WOUND."

"THE FAULT, DEAR BRUTUS, IS NOT IN OUR STARS, BUT IN OURSELVES, THAT WE ARE UNDERLINGS."

"COWARDS DIE MANY TIMES BEFORE THEIR DEATHS; THE VALIANT NEVER TASTE OF DEATH BUT ONCE."

"NOT THAT I LOVED CAESAR LESS, BUT THAT I LOVED ROME MORE."

"THERE ARE MORE THINGS IN HEAVEN AND EARTH, HORATIO, THAN ARE DREAMT OF IN YOUR PHILOSOPHY."

"BREVITY IS THE SOUL OF WIT."

"THERE'S A DIVINITY THAT SHAPES OUR ENDS, ROUGH-HEW THEM HOW WE WILL."

Four centuries after Shakespeare lived, to speak English is to quote him. His huge vocabulary and linguistic fertility are still astonishing. He has had a powerful effect on all of us, whether we realize it or not. We may wonder how it is even possible for a single human being to say so many memorable things.

Only the King James translation of the Bible, perhaps, has had a more profound and pervasive influence on the English language than Shakespeare. And, of course, the Bible was written by many authors over many centuries, and the King James translation, published in 1611, was the combined effort of many scholars.

EARLY LIFE

So who, exactly, was Shakespeare? Mystery surrounds his life, largely because few records were kept during his time. Some people have even doubted his identity, arguing that the real author of Shakespeare's plays must have been a man of superior formal education and wide experience. In a sense such doubts are a natural and understandable reaction to his rare, almost miraculous powers of expression, but some people feel that the doubts themselves show a lack of respect for the supremely human poet.

Most scholars agree that Shakespeare was born in the town of Stratford-upon-Avon in the county of Warwickshire, England, in April 1564. He was baptized, according to local church records, Gulielmus (William) Shakspere (the name was spelled in several different ways) on April 26 of that year. He was one of several children, most of whom died young.

His father, John Shakespeare (or Shakspere), was a glove maker and, at times, a town official. He was often in debt or being fined for unknown delinquencies, perhaps failure to attend church regularly. It is suspected that John was a "recusant" (secret and illegal) Catholic, but there is no proof. Many

scholars have found Catholic tendencies in Shakespeare's plays, but whether Shakespeare was Catholic or not we can only guess.

At the time of Shakespeare's birth, England was torn by religious controversy and persecution. The country had left the Roman Catholic Church during the reign of King Henry VIII, who had died in 1547. Two of Henry's children, Edward and Mary, ruled after his death. When his daughter Elizabeth I became queen in 1558, she upheld his claim that the monarch of England was also head of the English Church.

Did William attend the local grammar school? He was probably entitled to, given his father's prominence in Stratford, but again, we face a frustrating absence of proof, and many people of the time learned to read very well without schooling. If he went to the town school, he would also have learned the rudiments of Latin.

We know very little about the first half of William's life. In 1582, when he was eighteen, he married Anne Hathaway, eight years his senior. Their first daughter, Susanna, was born six months later. The following year they had twins, Hamnet and Judith.

At this point William disappears from the records again. By the early 1590s we find "William Shakespeare" in London, a member of the city's leading acting company, called the Lord Chamberlain's Men. Many of Shakespeare's greatest roles, we are told, were first performed by the company's star, Richard Burbage.

Curiously, the first work published under (and identified with) Shakespeare's name was not a play but a long erotic poem, *Venus and Adonis*, in 1593. It was dedicated to the young Earl of Southampton, Henry Wriothesley.

Venus and Adonis was a spectacular success, and Shakespeare was immediately hailed as a major poet. In 1594 he dedicated a longer, more serious poem to Southampton, *The Rape of Lucrece*. It was another hit, and for many years, these two poems were considered Shakespeare's greatest works, despite the popularity of his plays.

WHAT'S DONE IS DONE

SHAKESPEARE ON FILM: A SAMPLER

TODAY MOVIES, NOT LIVE PLAYS, ARE THE MORE POPULAR ART FORM. FORTUNATELY MOST OF SHAKESPEARE'S PLAYS HAVE BEEN FILMED, AND THE BEST OF THESE MOVIES OFFER AN EXCELLENT WAY TO MAKE THE BARD'S ACQUAINTANCE. RECENTLY, KENNETH BRANAGH HAS BECOME A RESPECTED CONVERTER OF SHAKESPEARE'S PLAYS INTO FILM.

Hamlet

Hamlet, Shakespeare's most famous play, has been well filmed several times. In 1948 Laurence Olivier won three Academy Awards—for best picture, best actor, and best director—for his version of the play. The film allowed him to show some of the magnetism that made him famous on the stage. Nobody spoke Shakespeare's lines more thrillingly.

The young Derek Jacobi played Hamlet in a 1980 BBC production of the play, with Patrick Stewart (now best known for *Star Trek, the Next Generation*) as the guilty king. Jacobi, like Olivier, has a gift for speaking the lines freshly; he never seems to be merely reciting the famous and familiar words. But whereas Olivier has animal passion, Jacobi is more intellectual. It is fascinating to compare the ways these two outstanding actors play Shakespeare's most complex character.

Franco Zeffirelli's 1990 *Hamlet*, starring Mel Gibson, is fascinating in a different way. Gibson, of course, is best known as an action hero, and he is not well suited to this supremely witty and introspective role, but Zeffirelli cuts the text drastically, and the result turns *Hamlet* into something that few people would have expected: a short, swift-moving action movie. Several of the other characters are brilliantly played.

Henry IV, Part One

The 1979 BBC Shakespeare series production does a commendable job in this straightforward approach to the play. Battle scenes are effective despite obvious restrictions in an indoor studio setting. Anthony Quayle gives jovial Falstaff a darker edge, and Tim Pigott-Smith's Hotspur is buoyed by some humor. Jon Finch plays King Henry IV with noble authority, and David Gwillim gives Hal a surprisingly successful transformation from boy prince to heir apparent.

Julius Caesar

No really good movie of *Julius Caesar* exists, but the 1953 film, with Marlon Brando as Mark Antony, will do. James Mason is a thoughtful Brutus, and John Gielgud, then ranked with Laurence Olivier among the greatest Shakespearean actors, plays the villainous Cassius. The film is rather dull, and Brando is out of place in a Roman toga, but it is still worth viewing.

Macbeth

Roman Polanski is best known as a director of thrillers and horror films, so it may seem natural that he should have done his 1971 *The Tragedy of Macbeth* as an often-gruesome slasher flick. But this is also one of the most vigorous of all Shakespeare films. Macbeth and his wife are played by Jon Finch and Francesca Annis, neither known for playing Shakespeare, but they are young and attractive in roles that are usually given to older actors, which gives the story a fresh flavor.

The Merchant of Venice

Once again the matchless Sir Laurence Olivier delivers a great performance as Shylock with his wife Joan Plowright as Portia in the 1974 TV film, adapted from the 1970 National Theater (of Britain) production. A 1980 BBC offering features Warren Mitchell as Shylock and Gemma Jones as Portia, with John Rhys-Davies as Salerio. The most recent production, starring Al Pacino as Shylock, Jeremy Irons as Antonio, and Joseph Fiennes as Bassanio, was filmed in Venice and released in 2004.

A Midsummer Night's Dream

Because of the prestige of his tragedies, we tend to forget how many comedies Shakespeare wrote—nearly twice the number of tragedies. Of these perhaps the most popular has always been the enchanting, atmospheric, and very silly masterpiece *A Midsummer Night's Dream*.

In more recent times several films have been made of *A Midsummer Night's Dream*. Among the more notable have been Max Reinhardt's 1935 black-and-white version, with Mickey Rooney (then a child star) as Puck.

Of the several film versions, the one starring Kevin Kline as Bottom and Stanley Tucci as Puck, made in 1999 with nineteenth-century costumes and directed by Michael Hoffman, ranks among the finest, and is surely one of the most sumptuous to watch.

Othello

Orson Welles did a budget European version in 1952, now available as a restored DVD. Laurence Olivier's 1965 film performance is predictably remarkable, though it has been said that he would only approach the part by honoring, even emulating, Paul Robeson's definitive interpretation that ran on Broadway in 1943. (Robeson was the first black actor to play Othello, the Moor of Venice, and he did so to critical acclaim, though sadly his performance was never filmed.) Maggie Smith plays a formidable Desdemona opposite Olivier, and her youth and energy will surprise younger audiences who know her only from the Harry Potter films. Laurence Fishburne brilliantly portrayed Othello in the 1995 film, costarring with Kenneth Branagh as a surprisingly human Iago, though Irène Jacob's Desdemona was disappointingly weak.

Romeo and Juliet

This, the world's most famous love story, has been filmed many times, twice very successfully over the last generation. Franco Zeffirelli directed a hit version in 1968 with Leonard Whiting and the rapturously pretty Olivia Hussey, set in Renaissance Italy. Baz Luhrmann made a much more contemporary version, with a loud rock score, starring Leonardo Di Caprio and Claire Danes, in 1996.

It seems safe to say that Shakespeare would have preferred Zeffirelli's movie, with its superior acting and rich, romantic, sun-drenched Italian scenery.

The Tempest

A 1960 Hallmark Hall of Fame production featured Maurice Evans as Prospero, Lee Remick as Miranda, Roddy McDowall as Ariel, and Richard Burton as Caliban. The special effects are primitive and the costumes are ludicrous, but it moves along at a fast pace. Another TV version aired in 1998 and was nominated for a Golden Globe. Peter Fonda played Gideon Prosper and Katherine Heigl played his daughter Miranda Prosper. Sci-Fi fans may already know that the classic 1956 film *Forbidden Planet* is modeled on themes and characters from the play.

Twelfth Night

Trevor Nunn adapted the play for the 1996 film he also directed in a rapturous Edwardian setting, with big names like Helena Bonham Carter, Richard E. Grant, Imogen Stubbs, and Ben Kingsley as Feste. A 2003 film set in modern Britain provides an interesting multicultural experience; it features an Anglo-Indian cast with Parminder Nagra (*Bend It Like Beckham*) playing Viola. For the truly intrepid, a twelve-minute silent film made in 1910 does a fine job of capturing the play through visual gags and over-the-top gesturing.

THESE FILMS HAVE BEEN SELECTED FOR SEVERAL QUALITIES: APPEAL AND ACCESSIBILITY TO MODERN AUDIENCES, EXCELLENCE IN ACTING, PACING, VISUAL BEAUTY, AND, OF COURSE, FIDELITY TO SHAKESPEARE. THEY ARE THE MOTION PICTURES WE JUDGE MOST LIKELY TO HELP STUDENTS UNDERSTAND THE SOURCE OF THE BARD'S LASTING POWER.

SHAKESPEARE'S THEATER

Today we sometimes speak of "live entertainment." In Shakespeare's day, of course, all entertainment was live, because recordings, films, television, and radio did not yet exist. Even printed books were a novelty.

In fact, most communication in those days was difficult. Transportation was not only difficult but slow, chiefly by horse and boat. Most people were illiterate peasants who lived on farms that they seldom left; cities grew up along waterways and were subject to frequent plagues that could wipe out much of the population within weeks.

Money—in coin form, not paper—was scarce and hardly existed outside the cities. By today's standards, even the rich were poor. Life was precarious. Most children died young, and famine or disease might kill anyone at any time. Everyone was familiar with death. Starvation was not rare or remote, as it is to most of us today. Medical care was poor and might kill as many people as it healed.

This was the grim background of Shakespeare's theater during the reign of Queen Elizabeth I, who ruled from 1558 until her death in 1603. During that period England was also torn by religious conflict, often violent, among Roman Catholics

ELIZABETH I, A GREAT PATRON OF POETRY AND THE THEATER, WROTE SONNETS AND TRANSLATED CLASSIC WORKS.

who were loyal to the Pope, adherents of the Church of England who were loyal to the queen, and the Puritans who would take over the country in the revolution of 1642.

Under these conditions, most forms of entertainment were luxuries that were out of most people's reach. The only way to hear music was to be in the actual physical presence of singers or musicians with their instruments, which were primitive by our standards.

One brutal form of entertainment, popular in London, was bear-baiting. A bear was blinded and chained to a stake, where fierce dogs called mastiffs were turned loose to tear him apart. The theaters had to compete with the bear gardens, as they were called, for spectators.

The Puritans, or radical Protestants, objected to bear-baiting and tried to ban it. Despite their modern reputation, the Puritans were anything but conservative. Conservative people, attached to old customs, hated them. They seemed to upset everything. (Many of America's first settlers, such as the Pilgrims who came over on the *Mayflower*, were dissidents who were fleeing the Church of England.)

Plays were extremely popular, but they were primitive, too. They had to be performed outdoors in the afternoon because of the lack of indoor lighting. Often the "theater" was only an enclosed courtyard. Probably the versions of Shakespeare's plays that we know today were not used in full, but shortened to about two hours for actual performance.

But eventually more regular theaters were built, featuring a raised stage extending into the audience. Poorer spectators (illiterate "groundlings") stood on the ground around it, at times exposed to rain and snow. Wealthier people sat in raised tiers above. Aside from some costumes, there were few props or special effects and almost no scenery. Much had to be imagined: Whole battles might be represented by a few actors with swords. Thunder might be simulated by rattling a sheet of tin offstage.

The plays were far from realistic and, under the conditions of the time, could hardly try to be. Above the rear of the main stage was a small balcony. (It was this balcony from which Juliet spoke to Romeo.) Ghosts and witches might appear by entering through a trapdoor in the stage floor.

Unlike the modern theater, Shakespeare's Globe Theater—he describes it as "this wooden O"—had no curtain separating the stage from the audience. This allowed intimacy between the players and the spectators.

THE RECONSTRUCTED GLOBE THEATER WAS COMPLETED IN 1997 AND IS LOCATED IN LONDON, JUST 200 YARDS (183 METERS) FROM THE SITE OF THE ORIGINAL.

NOTHING IN HIS LIFE BECAME HIM LIKE THE LEAVING IT

The spectators probably reacted rowdily to the play, not listening in reverent silence. After all they had come to have fun! And few of them were scholars. Again, a play had to amuse people who could not read.

The lines of plays were written and spoken in prose or, more often, in a form of verse called iambic pentameter (ten syllables with five stresses per line). There was no attempt at modern realism. Only males were allowed on the stage, so some of the greatest women's roles ever written had to be played by boys or men. (The same is true, by the way, of the ancient Greek theater.)

Actors had to be versatile, skilled not only in acting, but also in fencing, singing, dancing, and acrobatics. Within its limitations, the theater offered a considerable variety of spectacles.

Plays were big business, not yet regarded as high art, sponsored by important and powerful people (the queen loved them as much as the groundlings did). The London acting companies also toured and performed in the provinces. When plagues struck London, the government might order the theaters to be closed to prevent the spread of disease among crowds. (They remained empty for nearly two years from 1593 to 1594.)

As the theater became more popular, the Puritans grew as hostile to it as they were to bear-baiting. Plays, like books, were censored by the government, and the Puritans fought to increase restrictions, eventually banning any mention of God and other sacred topics on the stage.

In 1642 the Puritans shut down all the theaters in London, and in 1644 they had the Globe demolished. The theaters remained closed until Charles's son King Charles II was restored to the throne in 1660 and the hated Puritans were finally vanquished.

But, by then, the tradition of Shakespeare's theater had been fatally interrupted. His plays remained popular, but they were often rewritten by inferior dramatists and it was many years before they were performed (again) as he had originally written them.

THE ROYAL SHAKESPEARE THEATER, IN STRATFORD-UPON-AVON, WAS CLOSED IN 2007. A NEWLY DESIGNED INTERIOR WITH A 1000-SEAT AUDITORIUM WILL BE COMPLETED IN 2010.

Today, of course, the plays are performed both in theaters and in films, sometimes in costumes of the period (ancient Rome for *Julius Caesar*, medieval England for *Henry V*), sometimes in modern dress (*Richard III* has recently been reset in England in the 1930s).

PLAYS

In the England of Queen Elizabeth I, plays were enjoyed by all classes of people, but they were not yet respected as a serious form of art.

Shakespeare's plays began to appear in print in individual, or "quarto," editions in 1594, but none of these bore his name until 1598. Although his tragedies are now ranked as his supreme achievements, his name was first associated with comedies and with plays about English history.

The dates of Shakespeare's plays are notoriously hard to determine. Few performances of them were documented; some were not printed until decades after they first appeared on the stage. Mainstream scholars generally place most of the comedies and histories in the 1590s, admitting that this time frame is no more than a widely accepted estimate.

The three parts of *King Henry VI*, culminating in a fourth part, *Richard III*, deal with the long and complex dynastic struggle or civil wars known as the Wars of the Roses (1455–1487), one of England's most turbulent periods. Today it is not easy to follow the plots of these plays.

It may seem strange to us that a young playwright should have written such demanding works early in his career, but they were evidently very popular with the Elizabethan public. Of the four, only *Richard III*, with its wonderfully villainous starring role, is still often performed.

Even today, one of Shakespeare's early comedies, *The Taming of the Shrew*, remains a crowd-pleaser. (It has enjoyed success in a 1999 film adaptation, *10 Things I Hate About You* with Heath Ledger and Julia Stiles.)

THE "REAL" SHAKESPEARE

AROUND 1850 DOUBTS STARTED TO SURFACE ABOUT WHO HAD ACTUALLY WRITTEN SHAKESPEARE'S PLAYS, CHIEFLY BECAUSE MANY OTHER AUTHORS, SUCH AS MARK TWAIN, THOUGHT THE PLAYS' AUTHOR WAS TOO WELL EDUCATED AND KNOWLEDGEABLE TO HAVE BEEN THE MODESTLY SCHOOLED MAN FROM STRATFORD.

Who, then, was the real author? Many answers have been given, but the three leading candidates are Francis Bacon, Christopher Marlowe, and Edward de Vere, Earl of Oxford.

Francis Bacon (1561-1626)

Bacon was a distinguished lawyer, scientist, philosopher, and essayist. Many considered him one of the great geniuses of his time, capable of any literary achievement, though he wrote little poetry and, as far as we know, no dramas. When people began to suspect that "Shakespeare" was only a pen name, he seemed like a natural candidate. But his writing style was vastly different from the style of the plays.

Christopher Marlowe (1564-1593)

Marlowe wrote several excellent tragedies in a style much like that of the Shakespeare tragedies, though without the comic blend. But he was reportedly killed in a mysterious incident in 1593, before most of the Bard's plays existed. Could his death have been faked? Is it possible that he lived on for decades in hiding, writing under a pen name? This is what his advocates contend.

Edward de Vere, Earl of Oxford (1550-1604)

Oxford is now the most popular and plausible alternative to the lad from Stratford. He had a high reputation as a poet and playwright in his day, but his life was full of scandal. That controversial life seems to match what the poet says about himself in the sonnets, as well as many events in the plays (especially *Hamlet*). However, he died in 1604, and most scholars believe this rules him out as the author of plays that were published after that date.

THE GREAT MAJORITY OF EXPERTS REJECT THESE AND ALL OTHER ALTERNATIVE CANDIDATES, STICKING WITH THE TRADITIONAL VIEW, AFFIRMED IN THE 1623 FIRST FOLIO OF THE PLAYS, THAT THE AUTHOR WAS THE MAN FROM STRATFORD. THAT REMAINS THE SAFEST POSITION TO TAKE, UNLESS STARTLING NEW EVIDENCE TURNS UP, WHICH, AT THIS LATE DATE, SEEMS HIGHLY UNLIKELY.

The story is simple: The enterprising Petruchio resolves to marry a rich young woman, Katherina Minola, for her wealth, despite her reputation for having a bad temper. Nothing she does can discourage this dauntless suitor, and the play ends with Kate becoming a submissive wife. It is all the funnier for being unbelievable.

With *Romeo and Juliet* the Bard created his first enduring triumph. This tragedy of "star-crossed lovers" from feuding families is known around the world. Even people with only the vaguest knowledge of Shakespeare are often aware of this universally beloved story. It has inspired countless similar stories and adaptations, such as the hit musical *West Side Story*.

By the mid-1590s Shakespeare was successful and prosperous, a partner in the Lord Chamberlain's Men. He was rich enough to buy New Place, one of the largest houses in his hometown of Stratford.

Yet, at the peak of his good fortune, came the worst sorrow of his life: Hamnet, his only son, died in August 1596 at the age of eleven, leaving nobody to carry on his family name, which was to die out with his two daughters.

Our only evidence of his son's death is a single line in the parish burial register. As far as we know, this crushing loss left no mark on Shakespeare's work. As far as his creative life shows, it was as if nothing had happened. His silence about his grief may be the greatest puzzle of his mysterious life, although, as we shall see, others remain.

During this period, according to traditional dating (even if it must be somewhat hypothetical), came the torrent of Shakespeare's mightiest works. Among these was another quartet of English history plays, this one centering on the legendary King Henry IV, including *Richard II* and the two parts of *Henry IV*.

Then came a series of wonderful romantic comedies: *Much Ado About Nothing*, *As You Like It*, and *Twelfth Night*.

ACTOR JOSEPH FIENNES PORTRAYED THE BARD IN THE 1998 FILM *SHAKESPEARE IN LOVE,* DIRECTED BY JOHN MADDEN.

In 1598 the clergyman Francis Meres, as part of a larger work, hailed Shakespeare as the English Ovid, supreme in love poetry as well as drama. "The Muses would speak with Shakespeare's fine filed phrase," Meres wrote, "if they would speak English." He added praise of Shakespeare's "sugared sonnets among his private friends." It is tantalizing; Meres seems to know something of the poet's personal life, but he gives us no hard information. No wonder biographers are frustrated.

Next the Bard returned gloriously to tragedy with *Julius Caesar.* In the play Caesar has returned to Rome in great popularity after his military triumphs. Brutus and several other leading senators, suspecting that Caesar means to make himself king, plot to assassinate him. Midway through the play, after the assassination, comes one of Shakespeare's most famous scenes. Brutus speaks at Caesar's funeral. But then Caesar's friend Mark Antony delivers a powerful attack on the conspirators, inciting the mob to fury. Brutus and the others, forced to flee Rome, die in the ensuing civil war. In the end the spirit of Caesar wins after all. If Shakespeare had written nothing after *Julius Caesar*, he would still have been remembered as one of the greatest playwrights of all time. But his supreme works were still to come.

Only Shakespeare could have surpassed *Julius Caesar*, and he did so with *Hamlet* (usually dated about 1600). King Hamlet of Denmark has died, apparently bitten by a poisonous snake. Claudius, his brother, has married the dead king's widow, Gertrude, and become the new king, to the disgust and horror of Prince Hamlet. The ghost of old Hamlet appears to young Hamlet, reveals that he was actually poisoned by Claudius, and demands revenge. Hamlet accepts this as his duty, but cannot bring himself to kill his hated uncle. What follows is Shakespeare's most brilliant and controversial plot.

The story of *Hamlet* is set against the religious controversies of the Bard's time. Is the ghost in hell or purgatory? Is Hamlet Catholic or Protestant? Can revenge ever be justified? We are never really given the answers to such questions. But the play reverberates with them.

THE KING'S MEN

In 1603 Queen Elizabeth I died, and King James VI of Scotland became King James I of England. He also became the patron of Shakespeare's acting company, so the Lord Chamberlain's Men became the King's Men. From this point on, we know less of Shakespeare's life in London than in Stratford, where he kept acquiring property.

In the later years of the sixteenth century Shakespeare had been a rather elusive figure in London, delinquent in paying taxes. From 1602 to 1604 he lived, according to his own later testimony, with a French immigrant family named Mountjoy. After 1604 there is no record of any London residence for Shakespeare, nor do we have any reliable recollection of him or his whereabouts by others. As always, the documents leave much to be desired.

Nearly as great as *Hamlet* is *Othello*, and many regard *King Lear*, the heartbreaking tragedy about an old king and his three daughters, as Shakespeare's supreme tragedy. Shakespeare's shortest tragedy, *Macbeth*, tells the story of a Scottish lord and his wife who plot to murder the king of Scotland to gain the throne for themselves. *Antony and Cleopatra*, a sequel to *Julius Caesar*, depicts the aging Mark Antony in love with the enchanting queen of Egypt. *Coriolanus*, another Roman tragedy, is the poet's least popular masterpiece.

SONNETS AND THE END

The year 1609 saw the publication of Shakespeare's sonnets. Of these 154 puzzling love poems, the first 126 are addressed to a handsome young man, unnamed, but widely believed to be the Earl of Southampton; the rest concern a dark woman, also unidentified. These mysteries are still debated by scholars.

Near the end of his career Shakespeare turned to comedy again, but it was a comedy of a new and more serious kind. Magic plays a large role in these late plays. For example, in *The Tempest*, the exiled duke of Milan, Prospero, uses magic to defeat his enemies and bring about a final reconciliation.

According to the most commonly accepted view, Shakespeare, not yet fifty, retired to Stratford around 1610. He died prosperous in 1616, and left a will that divided his goods, with a famous provision leaving his wife "my second-best bed." He was buried in the chancel of the parish church, under a tombstone bearing a crude rhyme:

> GOOD FRIEND, FOR JESUS SAKE FORBEARE
> TO DIG THE DUST ENCLOSED HERE.
> BLEST BE THE MAN THAT SPARES THESE STONES,
> AND CURSED BE HE THAT MOVES MY BONES.

This epitaph is another hotly debated mystery: Did the great poet actually compose these lines himself?

SHAKESPEARE'S GRAVE IN HOLY TRINITY CHURCH, STRATFORD-UPON-AVON. HIS WIFE, ANNE HATHAWAY, IS BURIED BESIDE HIM.

THE FOLIO

In 1623 Shakespeare's colleagues of the King's Men produced a large volume of the plays (excluding the sonnets and other poems) titled *The Comedies, Histories, and Tragedies of Mr. William Shakespeare* with a woodcut portrait—the only known portrait—of the Bard. As a literary monument it is priceless, containing our only texts of half the plays; as a source of biographical information it is severely disappointing, giving not even the dates of Shakespeare's birth and death.

Ben Jonson, then England's poet laureate, supplied a long prefatory poem saluting Shakespeare as the equal of the great classical Greek tragedians Aeschylus, Sophocles, and Euripides, adding that "He was not of an age, but for all time."

Some would later denigrate Shakespeare. His reputation took more than a century to conquer Europe, where many regarded him as semi-barbarous. His works were not translated before 1740. Jonson himself, despite his personal affection, would deprecate "idolatry" of the Bard. For a time Jonson himself was considered more "correct" than Shakespeare, and possibly the superior artist.

But Jonson's generous verdict is now the whole world's. Shakespeare was not merely of his own age, "but for all time."

IF CHANCE WILL HAVE ME KING, WHY, CHANCE MAY CROWN ME.

A GLOSSARY OF LITERARY TERMS

allegory—a story in which characters and events stand for general moral truths. Shakespeare never uses this form simply, but his plays are full of allegorical elements.

alliteration—repetition of one or more initial sounds, especially consonants, as in the saying "through thick and thin," or in Julius Caesar's statement, "veni, vidi, vici."

allusion—a reference, especially when the subject referred to is not actually named, but is unmistakably hinted at.

aside—a short speech in which a character speaks to the audience, unheard by other characters on the stage.

comedy—a story written to amuse, using devices such as witty dialogue (high comedy) or silly physical movement (low comedy). Most of Shakespeare's comedies were romantic comedies, incorporating lovers who endure separations, misunderstandings, and other obstacles but who are finally united in a happy resolution.

deus ex machine—an unexpected, artificial resolution to a play's convoluted plot. Literally, "god out of a machine."

dialogue—speech that takes place among two or more characters.

diction—choice of words for tone. A speech's diction may be dignified (as when a king formally addresses his court), comic (as when the ignorant gravediggers debate whether Ophelia deserves a religious funeral), vulgar, romantic, or whatever the dramatic occasion requires. Shakespeare was a master of diction.

Elizabethan—having to do with the reign of Queen Elizabeth I, from 1558 until her death in 1603. This is considered the most famous period in the history of England, chiefly because of Shakespeare and other noted authors (among them Sir Philip Sidney, Edmund Spenser, and Christopher Marlowe). It was also an era of military glory, especially the defeat of the huge Spanish Armada in 1588.

Globe—the Globe Theater housed Shakespeare's acting company, the Lord Chamberlain's Men (later known as the King's Men). Built in 1598, it caught fire and burned down during a performance of *Henry VIII* in 1613.

hyperbole—an excessively elaborate exaggeration used to create special emphasis or a comic effect, as in Montague's remark that his son Romeo's sighs are "adding to clouds more clouds" in *Romeo and Juliet*.

irony—a discrepancy between what a character says and what he or she truly believes, what is expected to happen and what really happens, or between what a character says and what others understand.

metaphor—a figure of speech in which one thing is identified with another, such as when Hamlet calls his father a "fair mountain." (See also *simile*.)

monologue—a speech delivered by a single character.

motif—a recurrent theme or image, such as disease in *Hamlet* or moonlight in *A Midsummer Night's Dream*.

oxymoron—a phrase that combines two contradictory terms, as in the phrase "sounds of silence" or Hamlet's remark, "I must be cruel only to be kind."

personification—imparting personality to something impersonal ("the sky wept"); giving human qualities to an idea or an inanimate object, as in the saying "love is blind."

pun—a playful treatment of words that sound alike, or are exactly the same, but have different meanings. In *Romeo and Juliet* Mercutio says, after being fatally wounded, "Ask for me tomorrow and you shall find me a grave man." "Grave" could mean either a place of burial or serious.

simile—a figure of speech in which one thing is compared to another, usually using the word *like* or *as*. (See also *metaphor*.)

soliloquy—a speech delivered by a single character, addressed to the audience. The most famous are those of Hamlet, but Shakespeare uses this device frequently to tell us his characters' inner thoughts.

symbol—a visible thing that stands for an invisible quality, as poison in *Hamlet* stands for evil and treachery.

syntax—sentence structure or grammar. Shakespeare displays amazing variety of syntax, from the sweet simplicity of his songs to the clotted fury of his great tragic heroes, who can be very difficult to understand at a first hearing. These effects are deliberate; if we are confused, it is because Shakespeare means to confuse us.

theme—the abstract subject or message of a work of art, such as revenge in *Hamlet* or overweening ambition in *Macbeth*.

tone—the style or approach of a work of art. The tone of *A Midsummer Night's Dream*, set by the lovers, Bottom's crew, and the fairies, is light and sweet. The tone of *Macbeth*, set by the witches, is dark and sinister.

tragedy—a story that traces a character's fall from power, sanity, or privilege. Shakespeare's well-known tragedies include *Hamlet, Macbeth,* and *Othello.*

tragicomedy—a story that combines elements of both tragedy and comedy, moving a heavy plot through twists and turns to a happy ending.

verisimilitude—having the appearance of being real or true.

understatement—a statement expressing less than intended, often with an ironic or comic intention; the opposite of hyperbole.

SHAKESPEARE AND *MACBETH*

Title page of a nineteenth- ▶
century edition of the play,
from a wood engraving
after Sir John Gilbert

MACBETH.

Chapter
One

66929

Shakespeare and Macbeth

DURING QUEEN ELIZABETH I'S REIGN, ENGLAND BECAME A WORLD POWER, AND ITS PEOPLE PROSPERED. THE QUEEN DIED IN 1603. HER SUCCESSOR, HER THIRTY-SIX-YEAR-OLD DISTANT COUSIN JAMES I, LIKED DRAMA EVEN MORE THAN ELIZABETH. ONE OF HIS FIRST ACTS AS KING WAS TO MAKE SHAKESPEARE AND THE SHAREHOLDERS IN HIS ACTING COMPANY GROOMS OF THE CHAMBER. SHAKESPEARE COULD NOW DRAPE HIMSELF IN FOUR-AND-A-HALF YARDS OF SCARLET CLOTH PAID FOR BY THE CROWN. THE KING ALSO PICKED UP THE TAB FOR 187 PERFORMANCES OF SHAKESPEARE'S PLAYS IN THE THIRTEEN YEARS BETWEEN HIS SUCCESSION AND THE BARD'S DEATH. THIS WAS MORE PERFORMANCES THAN THOSE GIVEN BY ALL THE OTHER ACTING TROUPES IN ENGLAND PUT TOGETHER.

James I of England had been James VI of Scotland for twenty years before becoming king of England. Shakespeare honored James and his Scottish ancestry by writing *Macbeth* in 1606. He discovered the story in *Holinshed's Chronicles*, a popular history book at the time that also served as a source for a number of Shakespeare's other plays. But as he often did, Shakespeare made changes in the history to suit his own purposes. For example, he made the Scottish king, Duncan, old and venerable instead of young and weak. He also, for good reason, presented Macbeth's friend Banquo in an honorable light when he was originally part of the plan to kill Duncan. The real Banquo was the founder of the Stuart line, from which James I descended. Glorifying Banquo and then creating a scene where a long line of Banquo's descendants appear in one of Macbeth's hallucinations supported James's fantasy that his descendants would "rule over Britain to the end of the world."

Shakespeare reserved his biggest changes, however, for the character of Macbeth. In *Holinshed*, Macbeth is a one-dimensional warrior-type who served in a conventional way as king of Scotland for ten years. He's no shrinking violet in *Macbeth*, but he is capable of degrees of self-reflection, guilt, and remorse that the real-life ruler could probably never have imagined. Even though we may feel sympathy for the character, however, the play must have made a tremendous impact at the royal court for another reason. Only a year before its first performance, James's life had been endangered by the Gunpowder Plot, a failed attempt by Guy Fawkes and others to blow up Parliament and the king at the opening government ceremony on November 5, 1605.

Shakespeare also engaged the interests of James in another way: with the Weird Sisters. James was a big believer in and a respected authority on witches; he even wrote about witchcraft in his book *Daemonologie* (1599). A philosopher as well as a theologian, James oversaw the publication of the one book of his time that today rivals in popularity everything that Shakespeare wrote: the Bible that bears his name.

DOUBLE, DOUBLE TOIL AND TROUBLE

THE PLAY'S THE THING

- OVERVIEW AND ANALYSIS

- LIST OF MAJOR CHARACTERS

- ANALYSIS OF MAJOR CHARACTERS

A movie poster of the ▶
1948 film produced and
directed by Orson Welles

CHARLES K. FELDMAN
presents
ORSON
WELLES
in A MERCURY PRODUCTION
MACBETH
by William Shakespeare
introducing
JEANETTE NOLAN
with
DAN O'HERLIHY · RODDY McDOWALL
EDGAR BARRIER · ALAN NAPIER

Chapter
Two

66929
66929

CHAPTER
TWO

The Play's the Thing

ACT I, SCENE 1

OVERVIEW

Thunder roars and lightning crackles on a dark night above a Scottish moor. Three witches appear and plan to meet Macbeth after he's done making mincemeat of his king's enemies in battle.

ANALYSIS

What an opening! There is thunder and lightning to grab everyone's attention, and three eerie witches to stir King James's interest even more, since he was an authority on witchcraft. In addition to being riveting, this play is also going to be dark. Practically everything that happens in

Macbeth happens in the dark, which the Elizabethans feared even more than children do today. Nothing good ever happened in the dark. Darkness represented evil and the unknown.

The opening scene also mentions Graymalkin and Paddock, who are the witches' pets, called "familiars." They could take the form of anything from a toad to a cat. When witches were hanged or burned at the stake, their familiars often suffered the same fate.

ACT I, SCENE 2

OVERVIEW

A bleeding soldier tells King Duncan and his son Malcolm how bravely Macbeth and Banquo fought against the rebel Macdonwald and his Irish supporters. Macbeth sliced Macdonwald open from his navel to his jaws, cut off his head, and put it on the Scottish battlements. No sooner is the bleeding soldier carried off to have his wounds tended than a messenger arrives with news that Macbeth has also defeated the traitorous Thane of Cawdor and his Norwegian supporters (the word *thane* means "warrior-hero"). His throne saved, King Duncan proclaims Macbeth, the Thane of Glamis, the new Thane of Cawdor.

ANALYSIS

In the first scene we had darkness; now we have blood. And this is just the beginning. Dark and blood permeate this play. Macbeth's beheading of Macdonwald also foreshadows his own beheading by Macduff at the play's end.

ACT I, SCENE 3

Since we last saw the three Weird Sisters, one of them has been busy killing swine, and another is planning her revenge on a woman who refused to share the chestnuts she was eating. Now the three shrewish women have

AN OIL PAINTING BY JOHN EGBERT JONES, *THE WEIRD SISTERS*, DEPICTS MACBETH'S AND BANQUO'S ENCOUNTER WITH THE WITCHES IN ACT I, SCENE 3.

teamed up again to greet Macbeth and Banquo. When the brave soldiers appear, however, they shrink in horror at the sight of women with beards. Banquo says they don't look like "inhabitants of the earth."

The witches hail Macbeth as Thane of Cawdor, which puzzles him, since he has not yet heard about the honor that King Duncan has bestowed upon him. The witches then tell Macbeth that someday he will be king, and they tell Banquo that he won't be king but his descendants will. Before Macbeth can learn more from the witches, they disappear.

Macbeth and Banquo begin discussing the witches' strange prophecy, but they are interrupted by a messenger from Duncan, who tells Macbeth that he has been named the new Thane of Cawdor. The witches' prophecy has come true! Macbeth asks Banquo if he hopes his children will be kings, but Banquo cautions that sometimes "instruments of darkness" tell half-truths in order to cause harm. Macbeth ignores him. He's wondering if Duncan's crown will somehow fall into his lap or if he will have to do some dark deed to bring about Duncan's overthrow. As they are about to leave the heath, Macbeth tells Banquo that they should talk about what has happened at a later time. Banquo agrees "gladly."

ANALYSIS

In the previous scene, Macbeth was a brave warrior. Now Shakespeare has added another dimension to his character: His fascination with the witches' prophecy reveals an ambition so great he's willing to contemplate murder. Macbeth doesn't say that he will kill the king, but because this thought comes so readily to his mind, some critics claim that he may have already been thinking about it.

Also, the first words Macbeth speaks in the play, "So foul and fair a day I have not seen," echo the witches' statement from the first scene: "Fair is foul and foul is fair." Macbeth's words also underscore Banquo's warning that everything is not always what it seems.

ACT I, SCENE 4

OVERVIEW

At the king's palace, Malcolm tells his father, King Duncan, that the rebel Thane of Cawdor, whose title Macbeth has just received, has confessed his treasonous crimes and has been executed. When Macbeth and Banquo enter, Duncan thanks them for all they've done. Macbeth proclaims his loyalty to the king, and Duncan announces that his son Malcolm will be his heir to the throne. Macbeth pretends to be pleased with this news, but he realizes that Malcolm now stands between him and the crown. Plans are made for everyone to dine at Macbeth's castle that evening, and Macbeth leaves ahead of the others so he can tell his wife to expect company.

ANALYSIS

By opening this scene with the news of Cawdor's death, Shakespeare reminds his audience of the seriousness of the thane's crime. When immediately afterward the audience hears Macbeth wondering how he's going to deal with Malcolm now that Malcolm's been named heir to the throne, they cannot help connecting what Macbeth is thinking with the fate of the dead Thane of Cawdor. And that's not all. Cawdor's acceptance of his execution without resistance foreshadows Macbeth's resignation toward his own death, in the same way that the rebel Macdonwald's beheading in an earlier scene foreshadows Macbeth's own bloody end.

ACT I, SCENE 5

OVERVIEW

At the Macbeths' castle in Inverness, Lady Macbeth reads from a letter she has received from her husband. She learns of the witches' prophecies and regrets that Macbeth has the ambition but not the wickedness to take the shortest route to the crown. His nature, she says, is too "full of the milk of human kindness." What he needs is a push.

After a messenger announces that Macbeth is on his way and that Duncan will arrive later that evening, Lady Macbeth delivers her first telling lines. She begs the spirits to "unsex" her and says that if she were a man, she would kill the king herself.

LONDON'S OXFORD SHAKESPEARE COMPANY STAGED A 400TH ANNIVERSARY PERFORMANCE OF THE PLAY FEATURING A MALE ACTOR AS LADY MACBETH, IN KEEPING WITH THE ORIGINAL PRODUCTION.

Macbeth arrives. No sooner does he tell his wife that Duncan plans to spend only one night in their castle than she informs him that the king will never again see the sun. She advises him to "bear welcome" in his demeanor and to "look like the innocent flower" but be "the serpent under it." She'll do all the rest.

ANALYSIS

Lady Macbeth is one of the most amazing of all Shakespeare's characters, and we can see why in this scene. She dominates. No one in these early scenes—not the witches, the king, the soldiers, nor anyone else in the play—can equal the extent of her ambition, the intensity of her spirit, and the strength of her will. Her prayer to the evil spirits to make her masculine introduces Shakespeare's examination of gender roles. Is assassination, like war, the province of men? Is the role of women restricted to nurturing children?

Notice, too, how Shakespeare weaves into Lady Macbeth's words his images of darkness and blood. Duncan will never again see the light of day, a raven will announce his arrival, and, if Lady Macbeth's prayers are answered, the spirits will make the night "thick" like the darkest "smoke of hell." It will be so dark that Lady Macbeth won't see the wound her knife will make, nor will "heaven" be able to peep through "the blanket of the dark" and try to stop her. Lady Macbeth also prays that her blood, like the night, will be made "thick" so she will have no second (that is, feminine) thoughts about killing the king.

ACT I, SCENE 6

OVERVIEW

Duncan arrives at the Macbeths' castle with Malcolm, Banquo, Macduff, and others. The king describes the castle in words that emphasize its gentle beauty and sweet air. Banquo calls attention to the martlets—birds known for nesting in churches—that have chosen the castle for its similarly convenient corners and soft niches.

When Lady Macbeth welcomes the king and his retinue, King Duncan effusively thanks her for her hospitality. She replies, in equally extravagant terms, that the Macbeths' humble castle cannot hold all the honors Duncan has brought to it with his presence. Duncan then asks to be taken to the new Thane of Cawdor, whom he professes to love "highly."

ANALYSIS

Shakespeare is noted for his finely tuned sense of irony, and we see a perfect example of his genius at work in his description of the Macbeths' castle. Every word in this scene contrasts with what we know is going to happen before the night is over. Even the church-nesting martlets are juxtaposed with the battlement-dwelling ravens mentioned by Lady Macbeth in the previous scene.

ACT I, SCENE 7

OVERVIEW

Macbeth is not sure if murdering Duncan is such a good idea after all. On the one hand, there may be unforeseen consequences. On the other hand, he is Duncan's host, kinsman, and supposedly loyal subject. Furthermore, Duncan has done nothing to warrant an assassination. He is universally admired as a meek and virtuous ruler. In fact, the only reason Macbeth can think of to kill Duncan is his own "Vaulting ambition." When Lady Macbeth enters the room, he tells her, "We will proceed no further in this business."

That's what he thinks. Outraged by his decision, Lady Macbeth calls her warrior-hero husband a coward and says that the only way for him to prove he is a man is to kill Duncan. She has already come up with a plan. While Duncan is asleep, she will get his chamberlains drunk. When they pass out, she will take their daggers and, along with Macbeth, slip into the king's bedroom, kill Duncan, spread his blood on the daggers, place them next to the sleeping chamberlains, blaming them when the murder is discovered. Macbeth is so impressed with his wife's "mettle" that he tells her all her children should be males.

ANALYSIS

Because the Elizabethans believed that God—not people—gave kings their right to rule, to try to kill a king was not just a crime; it was also a grievous sin. Loyalty to the king was equated not just with loyalty to a sovereign or to a country but with loyalty to God. Macbeth says that he is not afraid of hell, but he doesn't want to turn into a monster, either. Isn't this what he means when he says he can do all that "may become a man," but any man "who dares do more is none"? If only Macbeth could meet Duncan on a battlefield where the killing is done quickly and without much thought. He's not cut out for taking someone's life when there's time to think about it.

Lady Macbeth, however, is definitely up to the task. She doesn't even consider Duncan's virtues, Macbeth's sense of loyalty, or the bravery her husband has shown in battle. She tells Macbeth that he will not be a man until he agrees to kill Duncan. By goading Macbeth into questioning his manhood, Lady Macbeth hits her husband right where it apparently hurts the most. Her statements also echo the sentiment that she expressed in that earlier scene, when she asked the spirits to make her a man so she could kill the king without any feminine thoughts getting in the way. Now she tells her feminine-thinking husband that, despite knowing the love that comes to a mother who is nursing a baby, she would rip her nipple from the baby's gums and dash its brains out rather than break a vow as he is threatening to do.

Rather than wilt under this attack on his masculinity, Macbeth rallies to his wife's conviction, constancy, and courage. Perhaps also thinking about

JOHN SINGER SARGENT PAINTED ENGLISH ACTRESS
ELLEN TERRY AS LADY MACBETH IN 1889.

"SCREW YOUR COURAGE TO THE STICKING-PLACE"

his royal lineage, he exclaims that all their children should be males, meaning that they all should have the same masculine, heroic, warriorlike qualities exhibited by his wife. And there's no doubt that he means what he says as a compliment. Her purposes may be sinful, dark, and bloody, but Lady Macbeth is a force unlike any Macbeth has ever encountered in battle.

ACT II, SCENE 1

OVERVIEW

Banquo and his son Fleance are walking late at night in a courtyard of Macbeth's castle. Banquo says that "cursed thoughts" keep him from sleeping. They unexpectedly run into Macbeth, and Banquo tells their host that King Duncan is asleep. He also says he's had a dream about the three witches and reminds Macbeth that there was some truth to their prophecies. Macbeth replies that he has not thought of the witches since they appeared on the heath, but suggests that he and Banquo discuss the witches' prophecies at a later time.

When Banquo and Fleance leave, Macbeth imagines a dagger floating in the air above him. Its handle juts toward him as if inviting him to take hold of it, while the tip of the blade points toward the room where Duncan is sleeping. Macbeth tries to grab the dagger and fails. He wonders if it is real or "of the mind." No sooner does he write the dagger off as a figment of his imagination, however, than blood appears on the blade. Suddenly a bell tolls. As Macbeth leaves, he says that the sound signifies Duncan's death knell.

ANALYSIS

Macbeth's meeting with Banquo and Fleance serves to remind us—and it should also remind Macbeth—of the witches' prophecy that Banquo's descendants will be kings. And, just in case we fail to make the connection, Banquo reminds Macbeth of the prophecies. Macbeth says that he never thinks about them. Nevertheless, he invites Banquo to talk with him later about what happened on the heath. Why does Macbeth do this? Could it be that he's trying to act as if nothing has happened since the men met the witches? Or might Macbeth have some role for his friend and comrade-in-arms to play in his new government? Or is it possible that Macbeth might be setting up a meeting so he can kill the only person other than himself and his wife who knows what the witches said? If Macbeth does plan to kill Banquo, his son Fleance will have to be a target, too.

ACT II, SCENE 2

OVERVIEW

Lady Macbeth waits for her husband. The wine that put the chamberlains to sleep has emboldened her, and everything seems to be going according to plan until her husband cries out from within the chamber. Either he hasn't found the chamberlains' daggers—which she put where he couldn't miss them—or the chamberlains are waking up before Macbeth can kill the king. She says she would have killed the king herself if old Duncan hadn't reminded her so much of her own father.

But, no, Macbeth returns, his hands covered with blood. He has killed the king. He tells Lady Macbeth that he heard the chamberlains wake up and then say their prayers before they went back to sleep. He had wanted to say "Amen" with them, but the sight of his "hangman's hands" kept the word from leaving his throat. Macbeth then adds that as he killed the king, he heard a voice cry, "Macbeth does murder sleep."

Lady Macbeth tries to calm her husband down by telling him that a little water will "wash this filthy witness" from his hands, but then she realizes that he's holding the daggers he used to kill Duncan and was supposed to place near the sleeping chamberlains. When she tells him to finish the job of setting up the chamberlains to be framed, however, he refuses to go back into the bedchamber. He says he cannot bear to look at what he's done. Accusing her husband of being "Infirm of purpose," Lady Macbeth grabs the daggers and heads off to where the chamberlains are sleeping.

ANALYSIS

Why did Shakespeare have Duncan die offstage? He knew how much Elizabethans, like Americans today, if modern movies are any indication, loved killing and the sight of bloodshed. He could easily have had Duncan murdered the same way he had Hamlet, Julius Caesar, and a host of other characters killed: right in front of everybody. Perhaps the reason is a practical one: If the dead Duncan were on stage when Macduff arrived in the next scene, the shock of discovery would not be as powerful as Shakespeare wanted it to be.

Might it also be that Shakespeare wants his audience to focus not so much on the murder as on something else, like the effect Duncan's death has on Macbeth? Macbeth's crime/sin is so horrific that he will never be the same. When Macbeth enters the chamber where Duncan is sleeping, he isn't afraid of hell; when he comes out, he blubbers that he will never again be able to sleep at night, and he refuses to go back inside to plant the bloody daggers in order to incriminate the chamberlains. How can it be that Macbeth, the Thane of Glamis as well as Cawdor—the one who led his army into hand-to-hand combat against the Irish, the Norwegians, and the rebellious Scots—is afraid to think about the murder he has committed and can't bear to see the king's dead body again?

Lady Macbeth tells her husband to wash the blood from his hands while she plants the daggers near the innocent chamberlains. After she's gone, there's a knock at the door. Macbeth notes how "every noise appalls" him. He says that if he were to put his bloody hand—the one that stabbed Duncan—into the sea, it would turn the water red. And that's not all. Macbeth's hands are not just the hands of an ordinary murderer. They're "hangman's hands." These kinds of hands had an added meaning for Elizabethans. Because hanging was almost as big a spectator sport as plays, the Elizabethans knew that hangmen didn't just string up their victims and cut them down after they'd died. They also disemboweled them and often cut their bodies up into pieces similar to the way Macbeth sliced and diced the rebel Macdonwald. Is this another foreshadowing of Macbeth's own end?

When Lady Macbeth returns to find her husband in the same emotional state as she left him, she points out that her hands are now just as red as his, but says she would be ashamed of herself if her heart was also as white as his. In her mind, "A little water clears us of this deed."

'TIS THE EYE OF CHILDHOOD THAT FEARS A PAINTED DEVIL.

KATE FLEETWOOD (LADY MACBETH) AND PATRICK STEWART (MACBETH) PERFORMED ON BROADWAY AT THE LYCEUM THEATER IN 2008.

At the sound of another knock, Lady Macbeth tells Macbeth to go put on his nightgown and stop thinking about what they've done. If only he could! If only Duncan could be awakened by the knocks on the door. But it's too late. Having done more than becomes a man, Macbeth no longer is one.

ACT II, SCENE 3

OVERVIEW

A porter, awakened from his sleep, responds to the knocking at the door, which he describes as "hell-gate" and himself as the "devil-porter." Macduff and Lennox, a Scottish nobleman, enter. When Macduff wants to know what took the porter so long to answer the door, he's treated to a dissertation on the effects of alcohol.

Macbeth enters, and Macduff asks to see the king. While Macduff is gone on this errand, Macbeth and Lennox talk about the nasty weather they've been having. Suddenly Macduff returns and cries out that a "sacrilegious murder" has taken place; Duncan's life has been stolen from the "Lord's anointed temple," as his body is called. Macbeth and Lennox run to the king's chamber to see for themselves. A bell rings shortly afterward, and everyone comes running—Lady Macbeth, Banquo, Prince Malcolm and his brother Donalbain, as well as other nobles and servants. "Confusion," as Macduff had predicted, "hath made his masterpiece!"

Confusion has little effect on Macbeth, however. In states of crisis, he doesn't have to do much thinking; he only needs to act. He kills the chamberlains, and when Macduff asks why, he says his reason was overwhelmed by his "violent love" for Duncan. Lady Macbeth faints, but that doesn't slow Macbeth down from doing what he believes he needs to do. While Banquo and Macduff see to it that Lady Macbeth is carried from the room, Macbeth calls a meeting of the nobles to discuss the next action to take. Macbeth has yet to be crowned, but already he's acting like the king. Prince Malcolm and Donalbain, meanwhile, conclude that as Duncan's heirs their lives are in danger and decide to flee Scotland: Malcolm goes to England and Donalbain to Ireland.

ANALYSIS

The appearance of the porter—many critics call it comic—may provide some relief from the tension that has been building toward the dark and bloody murder of Duncan, but not much. While his lowly station and his corresponding conversational tone of voice—as opposed to the iambic pentameter used by the nobles—indicate that he's not very important and probably doesn't have much worthwhile to say, the porter's words do contain statements that we immediately recognize as true. The Macbeths' castle at Inverness is no longer the sweet, pleasant, gentle, delicate nest described earlier by Duncan and Banquo; it's a living hell. And for all the confusion that reigns in Macbeth's mind, he might as well be drunk. He imagines daggers floating in midair, hears voices telling him that he'll never again have a peaceful night's rest, and can't remember to leave the incriminating daggers next to the sleeping chamberlains. The porter's final words—"I pray you, remember the porter"—are loaded with irony, since he has been referring to himself as Beelzebub and the Devil. And Macduff's appearance at the door is ironic as well. His knocks, which many critics view as death knells, foreshadow his killing of Macbeth.

The nasty weather taking place in the great outdoors, of course, is not ironic. It mirrors the dark confusion and bloody turmoil that's taking place in the castle. Lennox tells Macbeth that chimneys have blown down, screams of death fill the air, birds are shrieking, and the earth itself is shaking. Macbeth's response, "'Twas a rough night," has been interpreted by some critics as a sign of his distraction. Because he's thinking of the impending discovery of Duncan's body, he's not really listening to what Lennox tells him.

Saying that it is a "rough night" is an understatement. Macduff's use of the word *sacrilegious* and his description of the murderer as someone who broke open "The Lord's anointed temple" and stole "The life of the building" underscores the Elizabethans' belief in the divine right of kings. Duncan's death is nothing less than an attack on God's preordained governing structure. It's so grievous an offense that no word can describe it: "Tongue nor heart cannot conceive nor name thee!" Macduff exclaims.

No sooner does Macduff announce the murder of Duncan than Macbeth's course of action becomes clear. Becoming once again the nonthinking warrior-hero who defeated the forces of Macdonwald and Cawdor, he kills the sleeping chamberlains before anyone has a chance to question them. Not everyone, however, is convinced of the chamberlains' guilt. When Malcolm asks who murdered his father, Lennox replies that "Those of his chamber, as it seemed, had done it." *Seemed* is the key word here. Banquo and Macduff also have their doubts. They agree that, when the nobles meet, "this most bloody piece of work" should be investigated further, but nothing seems to come from their suspicions— not yet, anyway.

So much action (several battle scenes) and so many deaths (executions, assassinations, and murders) are taking place offstage, we have to raise the question again: Why is Shakespeare depriving his audience of the blood and gore they've come to expect from his plays? Some critics believe that he wants us to focus instead on the witches' prophecies, the state of Macbeth's mind, and the chaos that results from Duncan's death. Others suggest that Shakespeare is taking his lead from the Greek playwrights, who also kept most of their violent scenes offstage. Unlike the Romans and the British, the Greeks wanted their audiences to imagine violent acts through the verbal descriptions of the actors. They knew that the scenes that viewers imagined in their minds would have a more significant impact than any realistic representation produced on stage. Still other critics hold that Shakespeare was trying to please his biggest fan: King James I. James, as everyone in his court well knew, didn't like long plays, and *Macbeth*, which Shakespeare wrote in his honor, is one of the playwright's shortest.

ACT II, SCENE 4

OVERVIEW

Ross, one of Scotland's thanes, discusses with an old man the strange natural events that they've recently witnessed. The seventy-year-old man has never seen anything like it: An owl has killed a falcon, and Duncan's horses have gone wild and eaten one another. It's as unnatural as "the deed that's done," the king's murder. Ross agrees. The "heavens," he says, are "troubled with man's act," and threaten "his bloody stage."

When Macduff arrives, Ross asks him who "did this more than bloody deed?" Note the word *more*. A cautious Macduff answers, "Those that Macbeth hath slain." Ross has a hard time believing this. He says the chamberlains had nothing to gain. Again, perhaps not sure how much he can trust Ross at this point, Macduff tells him what the nobles have apparently concluded: that the chamberlains were bribed by Duncan's sons Malcolm and Donalbain and, having been found out, the brothers fled Scotland.

The nobles have also named Macbeth king, but Macduff will not travel to Scone to attend the coronation. He's heading to his home in Fife instead.

ANALYSIS

The purpose of this scene is to fill us in on the thanes' decision to name Macbeth king and to further the action of the play by informing us of Macduff's decision not to attend the coronation. But Shakespeare, as we well know, is never satisfied with merely providing updates or moving plots. Every scene is an opportunity to say something more than what is readily apparent. When Ross describes the "heavens" as being "troubled with man's act" and threatening "his bloody stage," for example, Shakespeare is referring to the underside of the roof that covers the stage. Known as "the heavens," it's decorated with stars and symbolizes the heavens where God resides. Shakespeare is telling his audience through Ross that God is not pleased with what he sees taking place on the "bloody stage" below him, and is letting the Elizabethans know of his displeasure through the unnatural events that are taking place in the Scottish countryside.

Macduff's decision to return to his home in Fife rather than attend Macbeth's coronation in Scone, moreover, is not just an indication of preference or a sign of fatigue. It is an insult to Macbeth that underscores Macduff's suspicions about who really killed Duncan. It also sets up the final confrontation between Macbeth and Macduff who, up until recently, has not figured prominently in the action of the play.

ACT III, SCENE 1

OVERVIEW

In the royal castle at Forres, Banquo can't help but think about the witches' prophecy that Macbeth would become king and Fleance would establish the royal lineage for years to come. The first part of the witches' prediction has come true, but Banquo fears that Macbeth has "played most foully" to bring it about. Banquo's thoughts, which hint at his own ambition, are interrupted by the Macbeths and other members of the royal court. The Macbeths invite Banquo to attend the feast they're hosting that night. Banquo accepts their invitation, but says he'll be away most of the day. If his horse is not up to it, he may not be back until after dark.

Banquo leaves, as does the rest of the court, and Macbeth asks a servant to show in the two men who have been waiting to see him. While the servant is fetching the men, Macbeth, as Banquo did earlier in the scene, reviews the witches' prophecies. If everything they said has so far

THERE'S DAGGERS IN MEN'S SMILES

come true, what reason is there to doubt the rest of their predictions? Did he murder Duncan just so Banquo's son could be king? Is he destined to wear a "fruitless crown"?

The men who have been hired to murder Banquo and his son Fleance enter, and Macbeth reminds them of a conversation they had the day before. He asks the men if they remember all the wrongs he said were done to them by Banquo. They do. Taking a page from his wife's book of motivation, Macbeth asks if they are manly enough to take their revenge on Banquo. They are. Will the men promise that, before the night is over, Fleance's soul will join his father's in its search for heaven? They promise that it will.

ANALYSIS

Scotland is quickly becoming an intolerable place in which to live. Macbeth killed Duncan to become king; he killed the chamberlains to blame the murder on them; now he has to kill Banquo and Fleance to prevent their family from ruling Scotland for generations to come.

And what about Macbeth's motivating the hired murderers with the same challenge to their masculinity that his wife used on him to bring about the murder of Duncan? What does all this talk about masculinity say about men? Is testosterone more powerful than friendship, loyalty, common sense, and God's will combined?

And why is Banquo planning to go riding with no destination mentioned on the day of the great banquet? Could he be thinking about following Macduff's lead in boycotting the feast and, at the same time, covering himself if he decides to show up after the party is over?

THE MACBETHS ENTERTAIN THEIR COURT AS KING AND QUEEN IN THE ROYAL SHAKESPEARE COMPANY'S 1993 PRODUCTION.

ACT III, SCENE 2

OVERVIEW

Lady Macbeth has discovered that murder has not brought happiness, or even a good night's sleep. It is better to be "that which we destroy" than "by destruction dwell in doubtful joy." Macbeth, when he enters, couldn't agree more. It would be better if he and Lady Macbeth were with the dead "Whom we, to gain our peace, have sent to peace" than torturing themselves with guilt. Their guilt notwithstanding, the Macbeths decide to murder the two latest threats to the throne: Banquo and Fleance.

In an earlier scene, Lady Macbeth told her husband to "look like the innocent flower" but "be the serpent under it." Now Macbeth tells his wilting flower of a wife that, as long as Banquo lives, they are unsafe. Once again, they must wear faces that disguise what is in their hearts and minds.

ANALYSIS

Macbeth talks a good game but, because his head is "full of scorpions," his voice lacks some of the conviction that Lady Macbeth's had when she persuaded him to murder Duncan.

What about Lady Macbeth? Is this the same woman who spurred her husband on to murder by demeaning his masculinity? Is this the same woman who said that the blood on Macbeth's hands could be washed away with a simple rinsing of water? Her tune has changed, too. She soliloquizes that "all's spent,/Where our desire is got without content."

ACT III, SCENE 3

OVERVIEW

Macbeth's murderers, now three in number, ambush Banquo and Fleance on their way back to the royal castle. Fleance's torch goes out in the struggle, but before the light in Banquo's eyes can be extinguished, he tells his son to flee.

ANALYSIS

Macbeth's ambition has spun out of control. Will he now have to kill the killers, too? And if he does kill them, whom will he hire to murder Fleance? And where did that third murderer come from? There were only two who met with Macbeth earlier in the day. Some critics believe that the unexplained presence of the third murder indicates that there might be some lines missing from the original text. Many cite this scene as an example of lines that Shakespeare didn't write. There's nothing in them but plainly stated action.

OVERVIEW

Before the planned banquet can begin, Macbeth has to meet with a certain person who is waiting for him with Banquo's blood on his face. Macbeth hails the man as "the best of the cut-throats," but becomes unhinged when he hears that Fleance has escaped. He feels "cabined, cribbed, confined," and "bound" to annoying "doubts and fears." Nevertheless, he tells himself that there's nothing to be afraid of; "the worm that's fled" has no teeth—yet.

Macbeth returns to the banquet, but there's a guest present whom he hadn't expected: Banquo's ghost. Not only has the ghost shown up uninvited, but he's sitting in Macbeth's chair. Macbeth talks to the ghost, but because he's the only one who can see the spirit, what he says doesn't make much sense to any of the guests. Ross concludes that Macbeth is not well and suggests that the party break up, but Lady Macbeth tells the nobles to ignore her husband. She explains that he's had these fits since he was a child and that this one will soon pass. Her first words to her husband are almost predictable: "Are you a man?"

What worked well in the past does not work so well now, however. Macbeth cannot get a grip on himself until Banquo's ghost leaves. But when the king raises his glass for a toast to "our dear friend" Banquo, the ghost returns, sending Macbeth once again into babbling that's just clear enough to raise the nobles' suspicions. Afraid that her husband might

WE HAVE SCOTCHED THE SNAKE, NOT KILLED IT

reveal their roles in the murders of Duncan and Banquo, Lady Macbeth takes Ross up on his earlier suggestion to cut the party short.

Alone with his wife, Macbeth claims that Banquo's ghost is out for blood. He has also learned that Macduff wasn't at the party, a signal that Shakespeare's audience would immediately recognize as treasonous. Before taking any action, however, Macbeth decides to talk again with the witches.

ANALYSIS

What is supposed to be a celebration of Macbeth's ascension to the throne turns into what Macduff predicted in an earlier scene: a masterpiece of confusion. And now there's no end in sight! Because Macduff has chosen to excuse himself from the banquet, Macbeth has a pretty good idea where his next challenge will come from and who his next target will be. But Macduff is only the latest person to reach the top of Macbeth's hit list. There's still the heir, Malcolm, in England and his brother, Donalbain, in Ireland. They have yet to develop the "venom" they need to kill, but they will. Not that it matters to Macbeth. He says he's already so steeped in blood that to wade through any more (don't forget about Fleance) would only make his return from the monster he's become to the human he once was—as if he could return—as "tedious" as the dark journey that has brought him to this point.

This brings us to Banquo. Why did Shakespeare choose to have Banquo's ghost make an appearance and not Duncan's? In *Holinshed's Chronicles*, Shakespeare's source for the play, Banquo is Macbeth's accomplice in the murder of Duncan. But in Shakespeare's version, he's an example of a man who, unlike Macbeth, can keep his ambition in check and whose descendants will establish a royal lineage for generations to come: right down to King James I, in fact. Critics who read *Macbeth* in terms of its historical context suggest that Shakespeare presents Banquo in a positive light because he wants to honor King James and keep those requests for royal performances coming.

ACT III, SCENE 5

OVERVIEW

Back at the heath, the three witches meet with Hecate, the goddess of witchcraft. She admonishes them for messing with Macbeth's life without first consulting with her. She tells the witches that she's in charge from now on, and instructs them to create illusions that will confuse Macbeth and lure him into a false sense of security, which Hecate tells us is "mortals' chiefest enemy."

THE WITCHES HOLD A GRUESOME PRIVATE MEETING IN A ROYAL SHAKESPEARE COMPANY 1987 PRODUCTION.

ANALYSIS

This time Hecate appears in a scene with the witches. Why? Did Shakespeare really need to include this scene in his play? If we need to know why the witches tell Macbeth what they do the way they do it in the opening scene of the next act, then the answer is yes. The answer is also yes if you believe that Shakespeare wants to engage James I's interest in a subject that is dear to him. Eliminating all but one of the visual representations of Macbeth's murders also allows Shakespeare to emphasize the unnatural and supernatural elements in his play. Witches, ghosts, imagined flying daggers, and more focus our attention on the moral decay and confusion that characterize Macbeth's dark thoughts as well as his bloody reign as king.

But there might be another reason still: Many scholars believe this scene was not written by Shakespeare in 1606 but was inserted at a later date for a special performance at King James's court and ended up getting printed in the First Folio in 1623.

ACT III, SCENE 6

OVERVIEW

Lennox and a lord discuss the state of Scotland. It's not a pretty picture. They know that the "tyrant" Macbeth is responsible for the murders of Duncan and Banquo, and the lord tells Lennox that Macduff has joined Duncan's son Malcolm in England to seek military help at the court of King Edward.

ANALYSIS

By including in his play the information that Malcolm and Macduff are seeking the aid of King Edward the Confessor, Shakespeare honors the strong bond of cooperation and mutual interest that has united England and Scotland for centuries. Thus, it becomes clear to the audience watching the play that Macbeth's murders involve not only Scotland but, as we see from the unnatural events taking place during his reign, the larger world as well. If nature is to be restored and the political chaos in Great Britain eliminated, Macbeth has to go.

ACT IV, SCENE 1

OVERVIEW

Macbeth meets the three Weird Sisters around a boiling cauldron and demands to know his fate. In response, the witches create several frightening and confusing apparitions: an armed head that warns Macbeth to beware of Macduff (Macbeth says he already knows that Macduff is his enemy), a bloody child who tells Macbeth that "none of woman born" shall harm him (Macbeth is relieved to hear this, but vows to kill Macduff anyway), and a crowned child holding the branch from a tree who tells Macbeth that he won't be vanquished until Birnam Wood moves to Dunsinane Hill (Macbeth is assured by the knowledge that the impossible can never happen).

As helpful as he thinks all these prophecies are, however, Macbeth has one more question: Will Banquo's descendants reign? A line of eight kings appears, with the last holding a mirror; the kings are followed by Banquo's ghost. The witches then disappear, and Lennox enters to inform Macbeth that Macduff has fled to England. Without a second thought, Macbeth resolves to kill Macduff's wife and children at their castle in Fife.

ANALYSIS

Who are these Weird Sisters? Their name comes from the Anglo-Saxon word *wyrd*, which means "fate," but are the witches' prophecies fate? The sisters are a powerful trinity, but how much control do they actually have over what happens? These are difficult questions to answer. Everything they predict comes true, but can they *cause* their predictions to come true? They know how to torment Macbeth, for example, but they don't seem to be able to harm him anymore than they could harm the sailor's wife who refused to share her chestnuts. Ironically, the witches, who come from the direction of hell if they enter the stage through its trap door, pose a theological question that the Elizabethans were very familiar with and that many Christians still debate today: If God is all-knowing, then he knows everything that is going to happen. If he knows everything that is going to happen, then the future is already determined. If the future is predetermined, then people have no free will. If people have no free will, then they are not responsible for their actions. Nevertheless, God holds them responsible. How fair is that? Shakespeare seems to address this paradox through the characters of the witches. They, like God, can see into the future, but their seeing into the future does not determine how Macbeth or Banquo will act. Banquo, like Macbeth, is ambitious, but he doesn't act on his ambition. He knows the boundaries placed on him by God. Macbeth, on the other hand, knows that murder is criminal and sinful, but goes ahead and kills anyway.

The witches' prophecies provide Macbeth with the false sense of confidence that Hecate insisted upon, but because we know that he is being deceived, we see the apparitions as signs that foreshadow the way the prophecies will be fulfilled. While Macbeth takes the witches at their literal word, we can only wonder how Shakespeare is going to make Birnam Wood come to Dunsinane. We know Macduff is going to end Macbeth's bloody reign, but how can he do it if he is not "of woman born"?

As for those eight kings lined up "to the crack of doom," some of them carry the three balls and two scepters that make up part of the royal insignia of Great Britain. The realization of this prophecy is reinforced by the king who carries the mirror. He not only creates, through its reflection, an infinite number of descendants from Banquo, but he can also reflect in the mirror the image of James I sitting in the audience.

Did Shakespeare believe in God or witches? We can't tell, and it doesn't really matter. What's important is what Macbeth believes.

ACT IV, SCENE 2

OVERVIEW

At her castle in Fife, Lady Macduff demands an explanation. She wants Ross to tell her why her husband has fled to England. Ross says that it isn't clear that he fled and begs her to have patience. She refuses. Her husband, she says, is a coward and a traitor who doesn't love his family. When Ross leaves, she tells her son that his father is dead, but the boy argues wittily and convincingly that he is not. Their clever repartee wins the audience's affection and, when a messenger interrupts them and tells them to flee for their lives, they win the audience's sympathy as well. After claiming that she has done no harm and, consequently, has no reason to flee, Lady Macduff immediately regrets her "womanly defense." That she has done no wrong, of course, is irrelevant. Macbeth wants her and her son dead. When the murderers enter, one of them calls Macduff a traitor. The boy, a chip off his father's block, calls the murderer a villain and a liar, but pays for his bravery with his life. Lady Macduff flees the room, with the murderers in pursuit.

WHEN OUR ACTIONS DO NOT, OUR FEARS DO MAKE US TRAITORS

ANALYSIS

Unlike Macbeth's earlier murders, which were committed to gain or retain power, no amount of reason can justify these killings. In other words, Macbeth has murdered simply to cause harm. According to his own definition, he is no longer a man but the monster he feared he would become if he murdered Duncan.

ACT IV, SCENE 3

OVERVIEW

Outside King Edward's palace in London, Macduff offers his services to Malcolm, but Malcolm says he doesn't trust the noble thane. He accuses Macduff of being Macbeth's ally and leaving his wife and children in Scotland, knowing that the tyrant wouldn't harm them. When Macduff refutes these charges and encourages Malcolm to fight for the throne that is rightfully his, Malcolm replies that, as bad as Macbeth is, he, Malcolm, would be an even worse ruler. He then lists many reasons why he would make "black" Macbeth "seem as pure as snow." Finally, Macduff can't take it anymore. He tells Malcolm that he is not fit to live, let alone govern Scotland. Malcolm then admits that he's been testing Macduff and now,

"STANDS SCOTLAND WHERE IT DID?"

convinced of Macduff's loyalty, is ready to place himself under the older and wiser man's guidance.

Ross arrives from Scotland. After first telling Macduff that his wife and children are well, he breaks down and admits that they have been murdered. Malcolm, again displaying the youth and inexperience he revealed through his absurd test of Macduff's loyalty, encourages the thane to take the news of his family's fate like a man. Macduff says he will, but first he must "feel it as a man."

ANALYSIS

Once again, Shakespeare asks us to consider what it means to be a man. The immature Malcolm associates manhood with a warrior's skills and attitudes, but the wiser Macduff tells him that there's more to being a man than aggression and killing. It's also important to feel pain, grief, and loss. This is advice that Malcolm needs to heed if he hopes to be a successful ruler of Scotland.

ACT V, SCENE 1

OVERVIEW

A doctor and a gentlewoman discuss Lady Macbeth's recently acquired habit of sleepwalking. Lady Macbeth suddenly appears carrying a candle. She imagines that there's blood on her hands and no amount of washing will remove it. She says, "Out, damned spot! Out, I say!" But there's too much blood for any amount of water to remove. "Who would have thought the old man to have had so much blood in him?" she asks herself. This is from the woman who earlier claimed that all it would take to clear her and Macbeth of their dastardly deed was "a little water."

The doctor comments that Lady Macbeth's disease is "beyond my practice," and the gentlewoman notes that she would not "have such a heart in my bosom for the dignity of the whole body." In short, Lady

Macbeth is beyond hope. Guilt and paranoia have done her in as assuredly as the chamberlains' daggers sent Duncan to his final rest. Her immediate recourse is to go to bed. Her final words of the play are "What's done cannot be undone."

ANALYSIS

The action is going to come rapidly to a close now. Instead of the longer preparatory scenes of the previous acts, a series of short scenes will lead to Macbeth's inevitable end. What holds our interest from here on out is discovering how the prophecies will be fulfilled, how Macbeth will die, and what will happen to Lady Macbeth.

ACT V, SCENE 2

OVERVIEW

As the rebellious Scottish lords gather their forces to meet Malcolm and his army coming from England, they report that Macbeth has fortified Dunsinane Castle for a siege.

ANALYSIS

This scene shows that the country's revulsion at Macbeth's crimes has caused many forces to unite against him.

ACT V, SCENE 3

OVERVIEW

Macbeth confidently dismisses reports that a large army is preparing to besiege his castle. As long as Birnam Wood remains in Dunsinane, he is safe. And isn't their leader, Malcolm, born of a woman? Defeat and death are impossible. But Lady Macbeth's descent into madness is not. When Macbeth asks the doctor if he cannot "minister to a mind diseased," he learns that the only person who can help Lady Macbeth is Lady Macbeth.

ANALYSIS

Remember the witch goddess Hecate telling us that security is mortals' biggest enemy? How right she was! Recall all that talk about how much better it is to have action done quickly. If only the Macbeths had taken the time to consider carefully the full consequences of their behavior. Now what's done cannot be undone; their fates are sealed.

ACT V, SCENE 4

OVERVIEW

Malcolm orders his soldiers to cut down branches from the trees in Birnam Wood and carry them to camouflage the size of his army as it marches toward Macbeth's castle at Dunsinane Hill.

ANALYSIS

The witches prophesied that Macbeth would not be defeated until Birnam Wood came to Dunsinane Hill. Those now-famous trees are about to make their trip. The "confident tyrant," as Lord Siward notes, is in for a surprise. We know what that surprise is, but we can't wait to see Macbeth's response.

ACT V, SCENE 5

OVERVIEW

Macbeth, wearing armor that he doesn't yet need, orders banners to be flown from his castle and boasts of his victory that is to come. But the bloodcurdling sound of women crying interrupts his reverie: Lady Macbeth has died. Shocked by his loss, Macbeth famously reflects on the meaninglessness of life. Life is, he says, "a tale/Told by an idiot, full of sound and fury,/Signifying nothing."

More bad news follows: The trees of Birnam Wood have arrived at

Dunsinane. Macbeth replies that he's beginning to grow "a-weary of the sun," but he vows to go down fighting.

ANALYSIS

Lady Macbeth has died, but how? Is it logical to assume that, given her psychological state, she has killed herself? Yes. Is this a conclusion that Macbeth could reasonably reach? Yes. Is it something the audience might assume? Again, the answer is yes, but it is not stated explicitly in the text.

We don't like Macbeth, but it's hard not to admire his courage. Even though he's become a monster, he will die like a man.

ACT V, SCENES 6 AND 7

OVERVIEW

Malcolm orders his soldiers to throw down their branches and mount their attack under the leadership of Macduff. In the midst of battle, Macbeth—confident that "none of woman born" shall harm him—is nothing short of a killing machine. One of his victims is Lord Siward's son. On another part of the battlefield, Macduff searches for Macbeth. If he can't personally avenge the murder of his wife and children, their ghosts will haunt him for the rest of his life. Malcolm and Lord Siward, meanwhile, prepare to enter Macbeth's castle.

ANALYSIS

Whatever deaths Shakespeare may have kept his audience from viewing—those of Macdonwald, Cawdor, Duncan, his two chamberlains, Lady Macduff, and Lady Macbeth—he makes up for in these last few scenes. And because most of the previous deaths took place offstage, there's no danger that the battle will seem anticlimactic.

SOLDIERS APPROACH MACBETH'S CASTLE IN A SCENE FROM ROMAN POLANSKI'S 1971 FILM.

ACT V, SCENE 8

OVERVIEW

Macbeth realizes that he has lost but refuses to "play the Roman fool" and die upon his own sword. As long as his enemies are standing, he's going to keep slashing. Finally, Macduff catches up with Macbeth, the "Hell-hound." Because he can't be killed by "one of woman born," Macbeth tells Macduff to fight those carrying "vulnerable crests." Macduff, however, has news for the tyrant: He "was from his mother's womb/Untimely ripped." Macbeth realizes that all the prophecies have now come true, but, as he vowed to do in an earlier scene, he dies fighting.

ANALYSIS

We don't have much compassion for the monstrous Macbeth. In fact, his death is something of a relief after all the bloodshed he caused. But we also can't help but admire his courage at the end and regret the extent to which it was wasted. His character is not without some sympathy. He realizes that his isn't a "charmed life." All the impossible prophecies have come true, his kingdom is in ruins, his wife is dead, and his time on earth is nearly over, yet he'd rather die fighting than suffer the public humiliation of kissing "the ground before young Malcolm's feet" and being "baited with the rabble's curse."

ACT V, SCENE 9

OVERVIEW

Lord Siward learns that his son died with his wounds on his chest, and Malcolm shows that he has learned a lesson about manhood from Macduff when he expresses his sorrow for the lost soldier. Macduff enters with Macbeth's head on a pole, and Malcolm invites all his loyal followers to his coronation in Scone.

Some texts do not introduce a new scene here, but instead have Macbeth and Macduff fight to the death onstage, with Macduff carrying Macbeth's body offstage before the arrival of the victorious forces.

ANALYSIS

Malcolm reveals his suspicion that Lady Macbeth took her own life. As the rightful heir to the Scottish throne, Malcolm sets the final tone of peace by promising that the disruption in the natural order that Macbeth has caused will be remedied in good time.

LIST OF MAJOR CHARACTERS

Macbeth: Scottish nobleman and officer in King Duncan's army

Lady Macbeth: Wife of Macbeth

Banquo: Scottish nobleman, officer in Duncan's army, friend of Macbeth

Macduff: Scottish nobleman, officer in Malcolm's army

The Weird Sisters: Three witches

ANALYSIS OF MAJOR CHARACTERS

MACBETH

Macbeth's reputation as a warrior precedes his entrance on the stage. Proud, brave, noble, successful in battle, and respected for his leadership, there is much to admire in him. We soon discover, however, that he is also superstitious and ambitious. Left to his own devices, Macbeth might not have acted on his ambition—at least not in ways that are inconsistent with being a loyal thane. But when he hears the witches' prophecy that he will be king, Macbeth doesn't know if he wants to wait for the crown to come to him. He may even have already been entertaining thoughts about murdering the virtuous, aged king to whom he is supposedly loyal.

Macbeth's ambitious thoughts turn quickly into action after Lady Macbeth questions his manhood, but he doesn't rush off to kill Duncan with the same intensity that he used to slay his king's enemies. He has reservations about killing someone who has been good to him and who is a leader who is much admired by the people of Scotland. Three times he hesitates to murder Duncan; he even refuses outright at one point. The reasons for Macbeth's hesitation are partly what prevent him from becoming one-dimensionally evil—like Iago in *Othello*—and allow us to sympathize with him to some degree, especially when we see how tormented he is by guilt and remorse. What keeps our sympathy in check, however, is Macbeth's lack of repentance—this and the fact that there is seemingly no end to the number of murders he will commit.

In addition to having a conscience, Macbeth has an active imagination. He sees flying daggers pointing the way to murder, oceans of blood that cannot be washed from his hands, and the ghost of one of his victims, which is as real to him as any living being. These hallucinations as well as his conscience have such a tight a hold on him that he can find relief from their torment only in action. In short, Macbeth is capable of the most horrendous violence—the murders of Lady Macduff and her children are an example—as long as he doesn't think about the consequences of what he does; conversely, he hesitates to kill King Duncan because he pauses to think beyond the crime he plans to commit. Unfortunately for his victims, Macbeth's guilt and remorse are never so torturous as to prevent him from taking innocent people's lives.

SOMETHING WICKED THIS WAY COMES.

When Macbeth hears the news of his wife's death, he is plunged into despair at the realization of what their ambition has wrought. Life without Lady Macbeth—and their love for one another is without question—is no longer worth living because it no longer has any meaning. Macbeth expresses this pessimism in what is perhaps the most famous speech in the play:

> LIFE'S BUT A WALKING SHADOW, A POOR PLAYER
> THAT STRUTS AND FRETS HIS HOUR UPON THE STAGE
> AND THEN IS HEARD NO MORE; IT IS A TALE
> TOLD BY AN IDIOT, FULL OF SOUND AND FURY,
> SIGNIFYING NOTHING.
> (V. 5.)

If only guilt, remorse, and pessimism were enough to allow Macbeth to admit defeat. But the word *defeat* simply isn't in his dictionary. His mind may be "full of scorpions," he may not be able to sleep at night, and his murders may have left him increasingly more isolated from the Scottish community, but his ambition to reign, his love of power, and his contempt for anyone that "first cries, 'Hold, enough,'" spur him to oblivion. Tragically—some even say heroically—he dies fighting for his life.

LADY MACBETH

Like her husband, Lady Macbeth is proud, courageous, and ambitious. But she's also more determined and ruthless. If she does have a conscience, she doesn't let it get in the way of whatever she wants to accomplish, at least at the beginning of the play. She even goes so far as to ask the spirits to "unsex" her so she can kill King Duncan herself and not have to rely on her equivocating husband. The spirits can't help Lady Macbeth, however, and she's forced to use traditional "feminine" methods to manipulate Macbeth into carrying out her will. When he resists her proposal to murder the king, she calls him the worst name anyone could ever call a soldier: "coward."

Then she taunts him with the suggestion that he is not a man and is not capable of becoming one until he kills Duncan. Any man who is secure in his masculinity, of course, would not be swayed by these arguments, but Macbeth cannot resist them because, like his wife, he associates manhood with violence and killing.

The strength of Lady Macbeth's will dominates almost every scene in which she appears. She compels her husband to kill Duncan, she calms his nerves after the dark deed is done, and she plants the bloody daggers on the innocent chamberlains. When Macbeth sees Banquo's ghost sitting in his chair at the royal banquet, it's Lady Macbeth who comes to his rescue. She explains to the nobles that her husband's behavior is an illness that has plagued him since childhood, cuts short his inadvertent revelation of the role he and she played in Duncan's murder, and sends her guests home before their suspicions can be roused any further. Even when she realizes the terrible consequences of their murders, she stays her course. And she does so like a trooper. She helps Macbeth but doesn't ask for his help; she listens to his complaints, but makes none of her own; and she appears to die by her own hand, rather than someone else's. Yet, like Macbeth, she also has her sympathetic side: She loves her husband, she can't stab Duncan herself because he reminds her of her father, she's tormented by the consequences of their deed, she is sickened at the thought of further killing, she doesn't blame Macbeth for what has happened to his kingdom, and her guilt is so great that it drives her to madness and, eventually, death. At the same time, like her husband, she never repents.

BANQUO

Banquo invites comparison with Macbeth. Also brave in battle, he praises Macbeth to Duncan even though the king didn't bestow upon him any rewards for his loyalty and valor. Almost as ambitious but not nearly so superstitious as Macbeth, he doesn't put too much weight on the witches' prophecies until he sees the effect they've had on his friend and comrade-in-arms. He warns Macbeth that "honest trifles" can betray deeper consequences, but he is in no hurry to discuss their futures, even after the first part of the witches' prophecies comes true. It's not until he and his son Fleance walk late at night through Macbeth's castle that his mood seems to darken. He complains that "cursed thoughts" have kept him from sleeping. Is he thinking about the witches? Probably. Does he think Macbeth may be plotting to kill King Duncan? Possibly. We can't say for sure, but when Macbeth says he killed the chamberlains out of "violent love" for his king, Banquo has his doubts. He's the one who suggests to Macduff that the nobles should meet to "question this most bloody piece of work."

Banquo is traditionally seen as one of the good guys in *Macbeth*, but he's not free of human frailty. Even though he's the only one besides Lady Macbeth to know of the prophecies, he doesn't discuss them with anyone after Duncan is killed. Nor does he take issue with the official view that Duncan's sons committed the murder. And, unlike Macduff, he attends the royal banquet celebrating Macbeth's accession to the throne. In other words, he keeps his ambition in check by not acting on it, but he does nothing to impede the progress of the witches' prophecies, either.

MACDUFF

Macduff is the model thane. Although he enters the play after the other major characters, he stands morally apart from and above them. It is Macduff whose four knocks on the door after Duncan has been murdered are often said to be death knells for Macbeth. It is Macduff who discovers Duncan's body and places the murder in the context of the king's divine right to rule. It is Macduff who, because he doubts Macbeth's innocence, boycotts the royal banquet. It is Macduff who counsels Malcolm on what it means to be a man. And it is Macduff to whom Shakespeare gives the honor of slaying the hated tyrant. In short, Macduff is the ideal warrior-hero and can always be counted on to feel with compassion and to do what's right.

He does make one costly mistake, however: leaving his family in Fife while he meets with Malcolm in London. Macbeth's senseless slaughter of Macduff's innocent wife and children extends the tyrant's cruelty almost beyond comprehension. There can be no sympathy for him now.

Lady Macduff, who contrasts with Lady Macbeth, is neither ambitious nor political. All she seems to care about is her family. Her anger at her husband's heading off to London, for example, does not include any consideration of what he obviously sees as a responsibility. Macduff's decision to leave his family was certainly a poor choice, but it wasn't an immoral one. In the end, he fulfills his duty to Malcolm and Scotland and avenges the deaths of his wife and children.

THE WEIRD SISTERS

Because we no longer believe in witches—at least not the kind that appear in *Macbeth*—we don't know much about them. Some critics say they refer to the three Fates of classical or Norse mythology—the Anglo-Saxon word for "fate" is *wyrd*—but the relation they bear to these spirits is in name only. Some critics say they help create the supernatural atmosphere that permeates the play, others say that they represent Macbeth's unconscious thoughts, and still others say that they're just a bunch of loonies who have been made noteworthy by Macbeth's superstitious beliefs. Whatever we might conclude, critics agree that the witches' influence on the play and on Macbeth is considerable.

To begin with, the witches can predict the future. Macbeth is named Thane of Cawdor, he does become King of Scotland, Birnam Wood does come to Dunsinane, Banquo's descendants do inherit the throne, and Macbeth is slain by someone not of woman born. But can the witches control the future? It's unlikely that Macbeth would have killed Duncan if the sisters hadn't predicted that he would be king, but the witches didn't force him to commit the murder. Had he been as patient as he was ambitious, Macbeth would probably have assumed the throne when Duncan died of natural causes. The king may have been virtuous, but he was also old. Of course, if that had happened, there wouldn't have been a *Macbeth*.

When Macbeth sees the witches after murdering Duncan and Banquo, he's a changed man. At their first meeting, Macbeth was brave and honorable—if a little too ambitious for his own good—and he knew the difference between right and wrong. He still knows the difference between right and wrong, but he doesn't care anymore. He hasn't had a moral hesitation since the night he murdered Duncan. In fact, Macbeth has become downright evil. And just to drive home the point of how little influence the witches have had on Macbeth's spiraling descent, Shakespeare has Macbeth commit an act that the sisters are not even aware of: the senseless murder of Macduff's family.

The witches spell disaster for Macbeth, not because they control the future (they don't), but because he believes in their ability to predict it. What he does with the knowledge they provide is up to him, however. Knowing the future, he also has the power to change it, for good or for bad. The criminal choices he makes are his, and, to his credit, he blames no one but himself. The witches may contribute to the dark and fearful sense of mystery permeating Shakespeare's play, but the tragedy is all Macbeth's.

A CLOSER LOOK

- THEMES

- MOTIFS

- SYMBOLS

- LANGUAGE

- INTERPRETING THE PLAY

A lobby card of ▶
Arclight Films' 2006
production starring Sam
Worthington as Macbeth

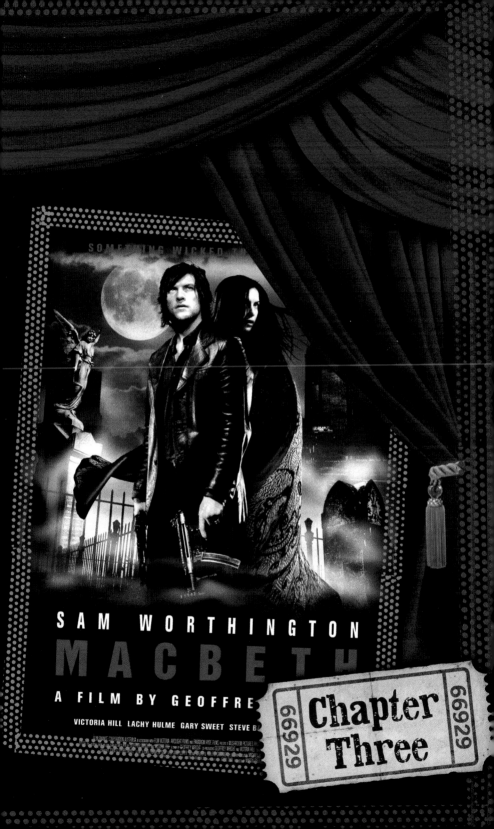

CHAPTER THREE

A Closer Look

THEMES

THE LESSON OF UNCHECKED AMBITION

The most obvious and probably least interesting theme of *Macbeth* is the lesson of unchecked ambition. It's one thing to fight for your king and reap rewards for your valor; it's quite another to kill God's chosen ruler and put yourself in his place. In fact, it's not just a crime but, according to the Elizabethan worldview, a grievous sin. After hearing that King Duncan has been assassinated, Macduff cries out against this "sacrilegious murder" and claims that the "life of the building" has been stolen from the "Lord's anointed temple."

What's interesting about Macbeth's ambition is that, until he meets the witches, he has kept it in check. He may have thought about overthrowing Duncan and seizing the crown, but he has neither said nor done anything to bring it about. Macbeth might have continued to harbor his fantasies even after his initial meeting with the three witches, but he happens to be married to someone much more ambitious and stronger-willed. For Lady Macbeth, the question of whether murdering the king may be right or wrong is irrelevant. Whatever it takes to secure the crown for her husband is the right thing to do.

When Macbeth kills Duncan, he unleashes what Macduff calls a masterpiece of confusion: "Confusion now hath made his masterpiece!" The natural order of the world—the one created by the Elizabethan God—is turned upside-down. The sun fails to shine, animals act in ways that are unusual for them, and the country is plunged into chaos until the Macbeths' guilt and remorse propel them to madness and their eventual deaths.

Perhaps more interesting than the Macbeths' unchecked ambition is the engine that drives it: love. The Macbeths don't love one another in the romantic way Romeo and Juliet do—when Macbeth returns from war, his wife doesn't even welcome him home with a kiss or a hug—but their unwavering support for one another and genuine concern for each other's success and well-being demonstrate that, whatever their courtship romance might have been, their relationship has matured into a partnership in the truest sense of the word. Unfortunately for Scotland, their focus is on power, and the result is murder, madness, death, and destruction.

THE UNSEXING OF GENDERS

The Macbeths' marriage presents another theme: what it means to be a man or a woman. This theme is relevant not only for the Elizabethans. The conventional womanly ideal may at first seem to be the apolitical Lady Macduff, who places her family above all other considerations. In this regard, she contrasts with her manly husband, who leaves his wife and children to join forces with the coalition that will overthrow Macbeth. But Lady Macduff is not totally content in her role as housewife and mother. When she's face-to-face with her murderer, she proclaims her innocence instead of picking up a weapon. Immediately, she regrets her "womanly defense."

Lady Macbeth also challenges the conventional definition of what it means to be a woman. She asks the spirits to "unsex" her so she can murder Duncan and not have to depend on her wishy-washy husband. But because she can't keep feminine thoughts from coming between her and murder—the sleeping soon-to-be victim reminds her of her father—she's forced to rely on traditional feminine wiles to motivate her husband to do the deed that she would like to do herself. At this, she is a pro. By calling her warrior-hero husband a coward and making a sexual connection in Macbeth's mind between murder and manhood—if he can't kill Duncan he isn't performing like a man—Lady Macbeth equates masculinity and sex with violence and killing. And because Macbeth also associates his image of what it means to be a man with what he would consider masculine forms of action, he finds in Lady Macbeth's challenge a greater motivation than his own considerable ambition.

Later in the play, when guilt and remorse have caused Macbeth to imagine that he sees Banquo's ghost, Lady Macbeth tries to help her husband regain some self-control by asking him, "Are you a man?" And in the final scenes of the play, Malcolm tells Macduff to "dispute" the murder of his family "like a man." Macduff, whose definition of *manhood* extends beyond that of the Macbeths', answers, "I shall do so,/But I must also feel it as a man."

What Shakespeare seems to be telling us is that sensitivity to others and feeling the pain of loved ones lost has as much to do with being a

OUT, DAMNED SPOT! OUT, I SAY!

man as any violence and though women may sometimes equal men in their desire to take the lives of others, they do not always have the emotional capacity. Not only that, but women who transgress in their traditional feminine levels of awareness run the risk, like Lady Macbeth, of descending into madness. When Malcolm bemoans the death of Lord Siward's son after the battle to overthrow Macbeth, he shows us that he has learned Macduff's lesson on the importance of sensitivity. Today we would say that Malcolm has gotten in touch with his feminine side. Because of this, we are led to believe that his rule as king will be marked by a compassion for others that is as much feminine as it is masculine.

MOTIFS

The major symbols (dark representing evil and blood representing violence) are also the play's major motifs. Almost everything that happens occurs in some dark place: the witches' prophecies on the heath, Banquo's walking around in Macbeth's castle because "cursed thoughts" prevent him from sleeping, Macbeth's sighting of the dagger that invites him to kill the king, the murders of Duncan and the chamberlains in their beds, the attack on Banquo and Fleance, the witches' apparitions in the cavern, Lady Macbeth's sleepwalking, and more. Almost every scene that comes to mind takes place in the dark, at night, or in poorly lit surroundings.Not only are the settings dark, but the language is as well. Macbeth tells the stars to hide their "fires" so light will not see his "black and deep desires."

Lady Macbeth asks the spirits to make the night "thick" so she won't have to see the wounds her dagger makes in Duncan's body. Nor does she want anyone in heaven to see what she's doing and attempt to stop her. The day after Macbeth murders the king, the sun has been strangled, and darkness entombs the face of the earth.

This is no ordinary darkness. It hides evil as well as any attempt to prevent evil from occurring. What kind of darkness is this? Perhaps it is a moral one. During her sleepwalking scene, Lady Macbeth insists that light continually be by her side. She thinks it can protect her from the dark thoughts that have come to infest her conscience since the murder of Duncan. Little does she realize that light, which is associated with what is good and right, only makes her more aware of the darkness of her deed. In other words, it illuminates rather than eclipses the blackness in her mind and heart.

On the one occasion when Shakespeare's "traveling lamp" does appear—on the afternoon of Duncan's approach to the Macbeths' castle—it signals that the world is at peace and all is as it should be, if only temporarily. Unaware of the dark plans being made inside, Duncan and his retinue soon discover that they've entered a living hell. The porter who answers Macduff's knocks after Duncan is murdered identifies himself as "Beelzebub" (the devil himself) and the door as "hell-gate." Are these not appropriate words to associate with Macbeth, whose valet's name, Seyton, is pronounced "Satan"?

And then there's the blood. Did evil night ever have a more appropriate companion? The word *blood* or one of its derivatives appears in the play more than forty times. The first person to enter the stage after the witches have delivered their eleven opening lines is a soldier wounded in Duncan's battle against the Scottish rebels and their allies. Bleeding from head to toe, he tells King Duncan how Macbeth sliced the rebel Macdonwald from his "nave to the chops," cut off his head, and mounted it on their fortifications. He is no sooner carried from the stage than word arrives of a second battle in which the combatants seemed to "bathe in reeking wounds."

And that's just the beginning! Lady Macbeth asks the spirits to thicken her blood so no feminine thoughts about murdering Duncan will reach her mind. Later, when tormented by the hallucination of the blood that she can't wash from her hands, she asks about the dead king, "Who would have thought the old man to have had so much blood in him?" Even worse

A NINETEENTH-CENTURY COLORED WOOD ENGRAVING DEPICTS THE MAD LADY MACBETH SEEMING TO WASH HER HANDS.

off is Macbeth. He's so steeped in blood that if he were to put his hand in it, the sea would turn red.

Macbeth's enemies would agree. Malcolm and Macduff imagine Macbeth holding a scepter covered with blood, and see Scotland as a bloodstained country that receives a new wound everyday. Blood permeates so much of the words and action of the play, in fact, that sights and images of it become almost routine. By the time Banquo's murderer shows up at the Macbeths' banquet with the dead thane's blood on his face, we hardly notice. And neither does Macbeth. He even goes so far as to praise the assassin as the "best of the cut-throats" and doesn't so much as flinch when he hears that Banquo's head is wearing twenty wounds as deep as trenches. What goes around, of course, comes around, and the last time we see Macbeth, Macduff has done to the tyrant's head what Macbeth did to Macdonwald's at the beginning of the play.

SYMBOLS

Underscoring the powerful motifs of darkness and blood is Shakespeare's symbolic use of nature. Before King Duncan's murder, nature is the way the Elizabethan God intended. None of the previous deaths mentioned in the play—and there have been many—has disturbed nature because all of the killings were morally justified. Even on the day of Duncan's murder, the sun is shining.

When the king and his retinue approach the Macbeths' castle, Duncan describes it as having a "pleasant seat." Banquo refers to the "delicate" air surrounding the castle as "heaven's breath," and calls attention to the birds nesting in the castle's "loved mansionry." These birds, called "martlets," usually prefer cathedrals. How symbolic is that?

The childless couple inside, of course, is neither the nesting nor the nurturing type. Lady Macbeth tells her husband that she'd rather pull a suckling child from her breast and dash its brains out than go back on a promise like the one he made to kill Duncan. She also asks the spirits to make the air in the castle as thick as the smoke in hell so Duncan can be killed before heaven can stop it.

After Duncan dies, nature turns as unnatural as the Macbeths' dark deed. Chimneys are blown down, screams of death fill the air, birds shriek at night, and the earth shakes. Even the sun's light is strangled. Mirroring the guilt-ridden confusion in the murderers' minds as well as the violent chaos soon to be wrought in their kingdom, an owl (which may symbolize Macbeth) eats a falcon (which may represent Duncan), and the dead king's horses break from their stalls as if they want to "Make war with mankind." Eventually, they eat one another.

So much for the animals and the birds. What about the plants? What symbolic role do they play? Banquo tells Macbeth to "Look into the seeds of time,/And say which grain will grow and which will not." In other words, Macbeth should decide what his future will be, and should not let the witches or anyone else define who he is or what he will become. This is good advice. Duncan tells Macbeth, "I have begun to plant thee, and will labor/To make thee full of growing." The king obviously has big plans in store for his thane. But Macbeth does not blossom in the way Duncan had hoped. His wife tells him to "look like the innocent flower,/But be the serpent under it." Toward the end of the play, when the Macbeths are reaping the bloody harvest they've sown, Malcolm tells Macduff that Macbeth "Is ripe for shaking."

Macbeth, too, describes his end in plant terms. He says toward the end of the play that his way of life has become a "yellow leaf," and that he cannot hope for the harvest that should accompany old age—"honor, love, obedience, troops of friends." His death, which will occur when the branches from those big plants in Birnam Wood arrive in Dusinane, is not far off. After Macbeth is defeated, Malcolm announces that Scotland has got to get busy doing that "which would be planted newly with the time." Nature's cycle, which starts in the play with the seeds mentioned by Banquo and ends with the new plantings by Malcolm, is now complete.

One final note: Macbeth dies childless and wifeless, but so does Macduff, who is portrayed as somewhat unnatural because he is not borne by a woman in the usual (vaginal) manner. He's also somewhat supernatural—what today we would call a "superhero"—in that he has no apparent frailties. His loyalty to Scotland, his ability to feel the loss of his family deeply, his advice about the importance of compassion to Malcolm, and his slaying of Macbeth—who, because he has nothing to lose, fights like a "hell-hound"—place Macduff in a supernatural hero class of his own. Loosely associated, but nonetheless associated, with Macduff's supernatural designation are the supernatural Weird Sisters. Their first set of prophecies anticipates the rise of Macbeth, but the second set—complete with an armed head, a bloody baby, and a crowned child carrying a branch—announces the coming of the savior Macduff as much as the fall of the evil Macbeth. Without Macduff, Malcolm would still be growing venomous teeth in England.

SHAKESPEARE EXPLAINED: MACBETH

"WHO DARES DO MORE IS NONE."

LANGUAGE

The importance of the role of language in Shakespeare's plays cannot be overemphasized, and any meaningful understanding and appreciation of *Macbeth* has to include Shakespeare's "poetry" as well as his plot. The thousands of people who flocked to the Globe Theater to see Shakespeare's plays were not called "spectators." They were an "audience," and, as the word suggests, they came to hear as well as to see. Because there was no scenery, no lighting, and only a few props, Shakespeare had to use his audience's ears to create in their imaginations what could not be physically represented on the stage.

The same is true for us today. To "see" *Macbeth*, we need to re-create the play on a stage in our minds. The words we read cannot just be a series of statements. They must be vivid representations of thoughts that we see as clearly as Macbeth sees the ghost of Banquo. So, when Duncan comments on his approach to Macbeth's castle, "This castle hath a pleasant seat; the air/Nimbly and sweetly recommends itself/Unto our gentle senses" that castle should appear in what Shakespeare calls our "mind's eye" as vividly as if it were on a motion-picture screen. Once we discover what happens in that castle, we can appreciate the irony that exudes from Shakespeare's exquisite description. In other words, it's Shakespeare's language that prevents *Macbeth* from becoming a relic of the past. It's Shakespeare's language that makes *Macbeth* come alive and continue to live on the imaginative stages of people's minds all over the world.

The people of Shakespeare's time, moreover, didn't shell out their hard-earned pennies to hear actors talk on stage the same way people talked in their homes or at work. They, like their Renaissance brothers and sisters throughout much of Europe, placed high importance on the beauty and power of words. They even had a name for it: *rhetoric*. Today we think of rhetoric as speech that is insincere or artificial. We might say, for example, that a politician's address to a crowd was "pure rhetoric." This was not the case in Shakespeare's time. For the Elizabethans, rhetoric was the art of persuasion through words.

The key word here, of course, is *art*. Shakespeare's characters were expected to say what they wanted to say in words that took ordinary language to a higher level. Their listeners wanted to hear not just *what* was said; they wanted to enjoy and admire the *way* it was being said. Notice how some of Shakespeare's characters refer to the immediate consequences of King Duncan's murder. Ross says that "dark night strangles the traveling lamp" instead of "The sun didn't come out." Macduff announces, "Confusion now hath made his masterpiece" instead of "It can't get much worse than this." When there is no single word to describe an event with the intensity Shakespeare wants to give it, he finds a way for one of his characters to express the feeling better than any single word could accomplish, even if it did exist. "Tongue nor heart cannot conceive nor name thee," Macduff cries out at the thought of what Macbeth has done. Is it any wonder the murderer can't sleep? His head is "full of scorpions."

Even Shakespeare's witches have a way with words. Here are a few lines extracted from one of their soup recipes:

EYE OF NEWT AND TOE OF FROG,
WOOL OF BAT AND TONGUE OF DOG,
ADDER'S FORK AND BLIND-WORM'S STING,
LIZARD'S LEG AND HOWLET'S WING,
FOR A CHARM OF POWERFUL TROUBLE,
LIKE A HELL-BROTH BOIL AND BUBBLE.
(IV. 1)

The words that the witches speak confirm their social position in the audience's mind. In a world where everything conforms to a strict hierarchal order, all the characters in all the plays can be identified and placed in the social order by the ways they speak. Their words are not only enriched beyond what any real person would say, but they often take on added, symbolic, even moral values. Take, for example, the witches' "Double, double, toil and trouble,/Fire burn, and cauldron bubble." The lines are clever, fun, possibly scary if you believe in witches, and structured to draw the audience's attention to the messages the witches are about to deliver. The lines are easy to write, easy to say, and easy to listen to. They don't engage our imaginations, however, in the ways that the lines spoken by many of the nobles do. Compare the witches' lines with these from Macbeth:

WILL ALL GREAT NEPTUNE'S OCEAN WASH THIS BLOOD
CLEAN FROM MY HAND? NO; THIS MY HAND WILL RATHER
THE MULTITUDINOUS SEAS INCARNADINE,
MAKING THE GREEN ONE RED.
(II.2.)

These lines are so highly structured (some would say "enriched" or "elevated") that they almost have to be read twice or even three times, not only to understand what Macbeth is saying but to appreciate the way he is saying it. If he were making a similar statement in a play written today, Macbeth might say, "Not all the water in the world can wash away the blood that's on my hand. In fact, I have so much blood on my hand that if I put it in the sea, the sea would turn red." But because he's a nobleman appearing in a Shakespearean play in 1606, Macbeth is expected to speak like someone who is high up in society. His words are what he is.

Read Macbeth's lines again and notice what Shakespeare has created through the words he's chosen to put in the king's mouth. The first line starts out with Macbeth proclaiming his guilt at having just murdered King Duncan. Can all the water in Neptune's great ocean wash away the blood that's now on his hand? The answer, of course, is a resounding "No." But Shakespeare doesn't stop here. He goes on to say that all the seas of the world will be made "incarnadine." Who but Shakespeare would choose to make an actor utter such a word? Didn't he realize that four hundred years after he wrote these lines, there would be people reading his plays who don't have time to look up in a dictionary all the words he didn't necessarily have to use? The groundlings, those penny-paying spectators in the pit of the Globe Theater, probably didn't know what it meant, either. But once we discover that *incarnadine* means "to make bloodred," we realize that not only can no amount of water wash away Macbeth's guilt, but Macbeth's guilt is so great that his hand (*incarnadine* also means "flesh-colored") would turn all the green color of the seas to red.

A LITTLE WATER CLEARS US OF THIS DEED.

Now, here's the best part. Can you see Macbeth looking down at his bloody hand? Do you notice how the guilty vision of the "incarnadine" line swells up almost like an ocean wave before receding in the third line the same way waves do? Shakespeare has created the feel of an advancing and receding wave in the very lines Macbeth speaks when he creates in our minds the powerful image of the sea turning bloodred.

Shakespeare uses language in yet another way. Because Lady Macbeth can't sleep peacefully at night, with her conscience ridden with guilt for all the terrible things she and her husband are responsible for, she sleepwalks through the castle and talks without realizing what she's saying. The words she speaks, however, are not the kind of "elevated" prose that Elizabethans would expect from someone in her noble position. When an actor didn't speak in character, the audience immediately knew that something was wrong. They didn't have to be told that Lady Macbeth—when speaking in a conversational tone of voice as she tried to remove Duncan's imagined blood from her hands—had gone mad. Her sentences, though rambling, are spoken in the ordinary, common prose of daily conversation:

> OUT, DAMNED SPOT! OUT, I SAY! ONE, TWO. WHY THEN, 'TIS TIME TO DO IT. HELL IS MURKY. FIE, MY LORD, FIE, A SOLDIER AND AFEARD? WHAT NEED WE FEAR WHO KNOWS IT, WHEN NONE CAN CALL OUR POWER TO ACCOUNT? YET WHO WOULD HAVE THOUGHT THE OLD MAN TO HAVE HAD SO MUCH BLOOD IN HIM?
>
> (V.1.)

When Shakespeare's audience heard Lady Macbeth speaking this way—as opposed to the witches' verses or Macbeth's "elevated" prose— they knew she had lost her mind. Why? Because she wasn't speaking like a noblewoman. By her behavior, the guilt that followed, and the madness that resulted, she had knocked herself out of her position in society. Once again, Shakespeare's lines say more than the words they contain. They become, in this instance, what Lady Macbeth no longer is.

Then, of course, there are the famous speeches. Imagine how Shakespeare's audience must have felt hearing Lady Macbeth utter these words while she waits for Duncan to show up at her castle:

> COME, YOU SPIRITS
> THAT TEND ON MORTAL THOUGHTS, UNSEX ME HERE,
> AND FILL ME FROM THE CROWN TO THE TOE TOP-FULL
> OF DIREST CRUELTY. MAKE THICK MY BLOOD.
> STOP UP THE ACCESS AND PASSAGE TO REMORSE,
> THAT NO COMPUNCTIOUS VISITINGS OF NATURE
> SHAKE MY FELL PURPOSE, NOR KEEP PEACE BETWEEN
> THE EFFECT AND IT. COME TO MY WOMAN'S BREASTS,
> AND TAKE MY MILK FOR GALL. . . .(I. 5.)

This speech shows just how determined Lady Macbeth is to seize Duncan's crown for her husband. She wants it so badly that she's ready to kill for it. But there's also something else going on. Lady Macbeth is asking her audience to consider what it means to be a man or a woman. Previously, we heard her husband doubt whether stabbing Duncan is a good idea; now we hear his wife not only praying to the spirits to give her the courage to kill Duncan herself, but associating the act of murder with her own sexual identity. "Unsex me here," she tells the spirits. "Come to my woman's breasts/And take my milk for gall." In other words, Lady Macbeth worries that her feminine instincts, which the breasts and milk represent, are going to stop her from committing the violent murder that men—her waffling husband excepted—don't have to worry about.

To enjoy *Macbeth* beyond the level of plot, we need to use Shakespeare's language to create in our minds a movie of what his Elizabethan audience heard, saw, and understood. We need to create on an imaginative stage the setting, atmosphere, action, and characters. We need to read the dialogue as a visual exchange of picture words. In fact, we need to be ready to leap at every verbal image that appears in what Hamlet calls our "mind's eye." We need to see this baby's brains splattering across the movie screen in our imaginations to appreciate fully how important it is that Macbeth keep his promise to murder Duncan when Lady Macbeth says:

> I HAVE GIVEN SUCK, AND KNOW
> HOW TENDER 'TIS TO LOVE THE BABE THAT MILKS ME;
> I WOULD, WHILE IT WAS SMILING IN MY FACE,
> HAVE PLUCKED MY NIPPLE FROM HIS BONELESS GUMS,
> AND DASHED THE BRAINS OUT, HAD I SO SWORN AS YOU
> HAVE DONE TO THIS.
> (I. 7.)

Similarly, when the servant informs Macbeth of the English Army's advance, we must "see" through our ears the two characters' fear and desperation:

> *MACBETH:* THE DEVIL DAMN THEE BLACK,
> THOU CREAM-FACED LOON!
> WHERE GOT'ST THOU THAT GOOSE LOOK?
> *SERVANT:* THERE IS TEN THOUSAND
> *MACBETH:* GEESE, VILLAIN?
> *SERVANT:* SOLDIERS, SIR.
> *MACBETH:* DEATH OF THY SOUL! THOSE
> LINEN CHEEKS OF THINE
> ARE COUNSELORS TO FEAR. WHAT SOLDIERS, WHEY-FACE?
> (V. 3.)

Only when we are able to let our ears be our guide will *Macbeth* be more than something that took place a long time ago in a language we no longer care about. Hamlet is right when he says, "The play's the thing," but the thing of the thing is Shakespeare's words.

"OUT, OUT, BRIEF CANDLE!"

Tomorrow, and tomorrow, and tomorrow
Creeps in this petty pace from day to day
To the last syllable of recorded time.
And all our yesterdays have lighted fools
The way to dusty death. Out, out, brief candle!
Life's but a walking shadow, a poor player
That struts and frets his hour upon the stage,
And then is heard no more. It is a tale
Told by an idiot, full of sound and fury,
Signifying nothing.
(V. 5.)

This is the most famous speech in *Macbeth*; it is also the most famous statement of disillusion and pessimism in the English language. It's so well done, in fact, that many people believe it to be Shakespeare's view of life rather than his tragic hero's.

Macbeth says these words when he learns that Lady Macbeth has died as he prepares for battle against the English. Some critics say that, given how much they loved one another, this passage doesn't express a whole lot of grief. Some say you could take this passage out of the play and no one would notice its absence. It contributes nothing to the plot or to our understanding of Macbeth as a character. Others feel differently. They claim that some pains are so deep as to be beyond words. In this sense, Macbeth's comments on the meaning of life are often said to demonstrate Shakespeare's enormous capacity to understand human nature. Because there are no words to adequately express his sense of loss at his wife's death, Macbeth doesn't talk about her at all. He chooses instead a subject for which he does have words. And what he says is not unconnected

A TALE TOLD BY AN IDIOT, FULL OF SOUND AND FURY

to Lady Macbeth. His words reveal in no uncertain terms the extent to which he has been undone by her death. Life is simply not worth living without her—or perhaps even living at all. It creeps along from day to day: "Tomorrow, and tomorrow, and tomorrow." Note Shakespeare's use of commas. We can't read the words quickly even if we wanted to. He literally makes the line creep tediously from one day to the next. Then there's the alliteration; "petty pace." Can you hear the contemptuousness in Macbeth's voice as he spits out the repeating "p" sound?

And where does this slow, petty, tedious repetition end? In "dusty death." So why not just blow out the candle that is already too brief? Does it matter how long we live? As full of "sound and fury" as Macbeth's life has been, it has amounted to nothing—unless, of course, you think that nothing can amount to something. Is Macbeth's history of murder, madness, death, and destruction any less terrible because it signifies nothing? If so, his tale may very well be that of an idiot.

It's also a tale told by an actor who "struts and frets" his hour on the stage. Does this mean that the significance we attach to Shakespeare's play is also an illusion? Or disillusion? Have we all—playwright, actors, audience, and so on—been participating in a reality that, like life itself, amounts to nothing? You decide.

INTERPRETING THE PLAY

Shakespearean criticism in the twentieth century starts out at a high point: A. C. Bradley. In *Shakespearean Tragedy: Lectures on Hamlet, Othello, King Lear, and Macbeth* (1904), Bradley—as the book's title suggests—focuses our attention on the main characters in each of Shakespeare's four great tragedies. What he says, basically, is that the central characters are so intelligent, brave, and strong-willed that only they and their individual tragic flaws, and not fate or chance, could have determined their unhappy ends. Bradley admits that fate, as represented by the three witches, influences Macbeth, but Macbeth is responsible for his behavior and all its terrible consequences.

What's particularly interesting about Bradley's analysis is that he treats Shakespeare's heroes as if they are real people, and not just characters in a play. So, when he reads how quickly Macbeth responds to the three witches' prophecy that he will be king, Bradley suggests that the thane had to have already been thinking about killing Duncan even before the play began.

Seeing Shakespeare's characters as real people—and don't we all do this to some extent with our favorite characters?—is also the focus of the criticism leveled against Bradley. Some scholars accuse him of seeing things in the text that aren't there. If popularity is any measure of insight, however, not many share this view. The former professor of poetry at Oxford University has been in print for over a hundred years—almost unheard of for a scholar.

The next influential critic to come along after Bradley is Sigmund Freud, the famous inventor of psychoanalysis. Because Shakespeare's works are so universally known and admired, Freud often used characters and scenes from them to illustrate his psychological theories. In fact, his idea for the Oedipus complex came to him while he was watching a performance of *Hamlet*.

For more than eighty years now, Freud's disciples have been putting Shakespeare's characters on their couches and analyzing them. From their point of view, those supernatural appearances of the witches in *Macbeth* are really the tragic hero's subconscious thoughts. The Weird Sisters' first prophecies are a classic example of the kind of wish-fulfillment that we create in our dreams. And what about those apparitions that we thought were created by the infernal triad toward the end of the play? They are symbols of the nightmare that is raging in Macbeth's mind: his most feared dreams come true in the worst possible ways. Unfortunately for Macbeth, he misreads the symbols.

Because he's not consciously aware of the thoughts that propel his behavior, Macbeth—though totally responsible for the death and destruction his reign has wrought—is not totally to blame. Or, at least, he is not without some sympathy. Much of his behavior has been determined by unconscious forces that are not only beyond his control, but of which he isn't even aware.

With the characters covered by Bradley and the Freudians, scholars have had to find other subjects to write about. In Shakespeare's use of images and symbols, they found a literary gold mine. Caroline Spurgeon, in *Shakespeare's Imagery and What It Tells Us* (1935), even goes so far as to create a profile of the character who created the characters: Shakespeare loved the outdoors, was probably good in sports, sympathized with animals, and feared disease.

The best of the image detectors, however, is G. Wilson Knight. He fills seven books with Shakespeare's images and what they mean. These images include animals, birds, sports, blood, disease, medicine, eating, drinking, water, sleeping, family life, night and darkness, light and sun, stars, religion, shelter, seeds, flowers, plants, trees, and more. In *Macbeth*, there are more than twenty-five images of clothing alone.

Some of the most interesting and least noted of the *Macbeth* images have to do with having children, being a parent, and establishing a line of descendants. The Macbeths don't have any children, Macduff's wife and children are all murdered, Siward's son is slain, Banquo's son escapes death, and Duncan's two sons are spared, with Malcolm set to become the next king of Scotland. Lady Macbeth has had at least one child—she says she knows the joy of a smiling baby suckling at her breast—but we don't know what happened to it. Macbeth is worried that his crown might be "fruitless," and Banquo has been told that his descendants will rule Scotland for generations to come. One of them, King James I, actually sat in Shakespeare's audience. And let's not forget those children who appear as two of the three apparitions the last time Macbeth sees the witches.

Enter the deconstructionists. Generally speaking, the deconstructionists tell us that, in every culture, there is a center of power. The people who are at the power center determine what is important for everyone else in the culture. Those closest to the center are the most important and most powerful, and those farthest away are the least important and least powerful. If you landed in the United States from another planet and observed how our society was structured, you might notice that men are more privileged than women, the rich are more privileged than the poor,

STARS, HIDE YOUR FIRES!

"LET NOT LIGHT SEE MY BLACK AND DEEP DESIRES."

white people are more privileged than people of color, heterosexuals are more privileged than homosexuals, English speakers are more privileged than non-native speakers, and Christians are more privileged than just about everybody else. In other words, rich, white, heterosexual, Christian men generally control most of the power in this country, and those who look, think, and act like these men make up most of the power elite. The powerful may celebrate or at least tolerate the differences that exist away from the center, but they do so only insofar as those who are different and marginalized don't threaten them.

A similar structure is in place for the characters who inhabit the world of *Macbeth*: Because thanes hold most of the power, they are more privileged than any attendants; men are valued more highly than women; war, which is determined by thanes and fought by soldiers, is held in higher esteem than negotiation; and monarchies—God's choice for civic rule—are considered more effective than democracies.

Deconstructionists encourage us to break down (deconstruct) power centers into their individual parts so their deeper meanings can be understood. Instead of presenting thanes, ladies, monarchs, and attendants as parts of a unified, holistic culture, the deconstructionists show us how the Elizabethan world is divided into fragments that are either at odds with one another or would be at odds if the people within those fragments knew how oppressed they were. In other words, each fragment is characterized by its own individual differences, and the people within each fragment either resent, resist, and rebel—or should be resenting, resisting, and rebelling—against the forces that restrict them. All, that is, except those who are at the very center of power. They have nothing to rebel against; their job is to keep the existing power structure in place by subduing the resentment, resistance, and rebellions of everybody else. From this perspective, Shakespeare is seen not as an advocate of, say, women's liberation—Lady Macbeth is often praised in feminist circles as an independent-minded, strong-willed woman—but as a supporter of the Elizabethan status quo, with men making the final decisions and women, because of their status and conditioning, having to rely on their wiles to manipulate men into doing their bidding. And that's not all. Reading Shakespeare's plays to fulfill school assignments today is cited by deconstructionists as an example of how the American educational system supports the country's right-wing agenda.

Whether the deconstructionists confirm or challenge your viewpoints of Elizabethan and/or contemporary American culture, to think about *Macbeth* is to become a participant in the creative process that Shakespeare began in 1603. It may be his words on the page, but it's your picture in your mind. How you see that picture, what it means to you, and what about it you believe is significant enough to share with others, are all creative acts. In short, once you've read *Macbeth*, the play not only becomes a part of you, you become a part of it.

Chronology

1564	William Shakespeare is born on April 23 in Stratford-upon-Avon, England
1578–1582	Span of Shakespeare's "Lost Years," covering the time between leaving school and marrying Anne Hathaway of Stratford
1582	At age eighteen Shakespeare marries Anne Hathaway, age twenty-six, on November 28
1583	Susanna Shakespeare, William and Anne's first child, is born in May, six months after the wedding
1584	Birth of twins Hamnet and Judith Shakespeare
1585–1592	Shakespeare leaves his family in Stratford to become an actor and playwright in a London theater company
1587	Public beheading of Mary Queen of Scots
1593–94	The Bubonic (Black) Plague closes theaters in London
1594–96	As a leading playwright, Shakespeare creates some of his most popular work, including *A Midsummer Night's Dream* and *Romeo and Juliet*
1596	Hamnet Shakespeare dies in August at age eleven, possibly of plague

1596–97	*The Merchant of Venice* and *Henry IV, Part One* most likely are written
1599	The Globe Theater opens
1600	*Julius Caesar* is first performed at the Globe
1600–01	*Hamlet* is believed to have been written
1601–02	*Twelfth Night* is probably composed
1603	Queen Elizabeth dies; Scottish king James VI succeeds her and becomes England's James I
1604	Shakespeare pens *Othello*
1605	*Macbeth* is composed
1608–1610	London's theaters are forced to close when the plague returns and kills an estimated 33,000 people
1611	*The Tempest* is written
1613	The Globe Theater is destroyed by fire
1614	Reopening of the Globe
1616	Shakespeare dies on April 23
1623	Anne Hathaway, Shakespeare's widow, dies; a collection of Shakespeare's plays, known as the First Folio, is published

Source Notes

p. 38, par. 1, 187 performances. Brian Bryson. *Shakespeare: The World as Stage.* (New York: Harper Collins, 2007), p. 134.

p. 50, par. 1, Most Elizabethans believed in a system of thought known as the Great Chain of Being. They saw the whole world as a kind of chain, or ladder, with God at the very top and rocks at the very bottom. Everything created by God had its place and purpose somewhere on the chain. People, for example, were below the angels in order of importance in God's mind but above the animals. Similarly, people born into royalty were considered to be more important than common people. To overthrow a king who was believed to rule by "divine right" was to commit the most grievous sin—pride. Pride meant you thought you knew better than God. Because pride is the sin that leads to Adam and Eve being expelled from the Garden of Eden, some scholars liken the Macbeths to Adam and Eve.

p. 59, par. 2, Critics influenced by the psychoanalytical theories of Sigmund Freud point out the forces at work within Macbeth's mind that he's not consciously aware of. Here's John Lahr of *The New Yorker* commenting on a production of *Macbeth* appearing on Broadway at the time of this writing: "Goold [the director] stages the three Weird Sisters as their psychologically astute author intuited them to be—as incarnations of Macbeth's unconscious." (3 March 2008, p. 84)

p. 66, par. 3, Frank Kermode. "Introduction to *Macbeth,*" *The Riverside Shakespeare*, Second Edition. (Boston: Houghton Mifflin, 1997), p. 1356.

p. 84, par. 3, Norman Holland. *The Shakespearean Imagination.* (New York: Macmillan, 1964), pp. 50–51.

p. 88, par. 1, See above notes for p. 13, par. 2. The murder of Duncan is "sacrilegious" because God has "chosen" him to rule Scotland.

p. 89, par. 2, See previous notes for p. 50, par.1. When God's order is disrupted by a grievous sin, it is not uncommon in literature for nature to reflect the chaos that results.

p. 92, par. 3, Holland. *The Shakespearean Imagination*, pp. 46–47.

p. 94, par. 2, Before King Duncan's murder, everything is in its place in the Great Chain of Being (see previous notes for p. 50, par. 1). With God's choice of king sitting on the throne and the Scottish rebels defeated, Macbeth's castle is likened to a cathedral in which gentle birds build their nests.

p. 99, par. 1, Harry Levin. "The Linguistic Medium" from the "General Introduction" to *The Riverside Shakespeare*, pp. 8–11.

p. 104, par. 2, Holland. *The Shakespearean Imagination*, p. 68. "Take, for example, what is probably the most famous speech in *Macbeth*.... Shakespeare could perfectly well have left it out, and it doesn't seem to have a great deal to do with the immediate occasion for the speech, Lady Macbeth's death."

p. 106, par. 1, Bradley, A. C. *Shakespearean Tragedy: Lectures on Hamlet, Othello, King Lear, and Macbeth.* (New York: Palgrave Macmillan, 2007), pp. 289–303.

p. 107, par. 1, Freud's influence is cited by Harry Levin in "Ernest Jones and Psychoanalytic Criticism," from the "General Introduction" to *The Riverside Shakespeare*, pp. 32–33.

p. 107, par. 3, Spurgeon's conclusions are cited by Harry Levin in "G. Wilson Knight and the Analysis of Image and Theme," from the "General Introduction" to *The Riverside Shakespeare*, pp. 33–34.

p. 107, par. 4, Knight's contribution to Shakespeare's use of images is most prominent in *The Wheel of Fire: Interpretations of Shakespearean Tragedy.* (New York: Routledge, 2001).

A Shakespeare Glossary

The student should not try to memorize these, but only refer to them as needed. We can never stress enough that the best way to learn Shakespeare's language is simply to *hear* it—to hear it spoken well by good actors. After all, small children master every language on earth through their ears, without studying dictionaries, and we should master Shakespeare, as much as possible, the same way.

addition —a name or title (knight, duke, duchess, king, etc.)

admire —to marvel

affect —to like or love; to be attracted to

an —if ("An I tell you that, I'll be hanged.")

approve —to prove or confirm

attend —to pay attention

belike —probably

beseech —to beg or request

betimes —soon; early

bondman —a slave

bootless —futile; useless; in vain

broil —a battle

charge —expense, responsibility; to command or accuse

clepe, clept —to name; named

common —of the common people; below the nobility

conceit —imagination

condition —social rank; quality

countenance —face; appearance; favor

cousin —a relative

cry you mercy —beg your pardon

curious —careful; attentive to detail

dear —expensive

discourse —to converse; conversation

discover —to reveal or uncover

dispatch —to speed or hurry; to send; to kill

doubt —to suspect

entreat —to beg or appeal

envy —to hate or resent; hatred; resentment

ere —before

ever, e'er —always

eyne —eyes

fain —gladly

fare —to eat; to prosper

favor —face, privilege

fellow —a peer or equal

filial —of a child toward its parent

fine —an end; in fine = in sum

fond —foolish

fool —a darling

genius —a good or evil spirit

gentle —well-bred; not common;

gentleman —one whose labor was done by servants (Note: to call someone a *gentleman* was not a mere compliment on his manners; it meant that he was above the common people.)

gentles —people of quality

get —to beget (a child)

go to —"go on"; "come off it"

go we —let us go

haply —perhaps

happily —by chance; fortunately

hard by —nearby

heavy —sad or serious

husbandry —thrift; economy

instant —immediate

kind —one's nature; species

knave —a villain; a poor man

lady —a woman of high social rank (Note: *lady* was not a synonym for *woman* or *polite woman*; it was not a compliment, but, like *gentleman*, simply a word referring to one's actual legal status in society.)

leave — permission; "take my leave" = depart (with permission)

lief, lieve — "I had as lief" = I would just as soon; I would rather

like —to please; "it likes me not" = it is disagreeable to me

livery —the uniform of a nobleman's servants; emblem

mark —notice; pay attention

morrow —morning

needs —necessarily

nice —too fussy or fastidious

owe —to own

passing —very

peculiar —individual; exclusive

privy —private; secret

proper —handsome; one's very own ("his proper son")

protest —to insist or declare

quite —completely

require —request

several —different, various;

severally —separately

sirrah —a term used to address social inferiors

sooth —truth

state —condition; social rank

still —always; persistently

success —result(s)

surfeit —fullness

touching —concerning; about; as for

translate —to transform

unfold —to disclose

villain —a low or evil person; originally, a peasant

voice —a vote; consent; approval

vouchsafe —to confide or grant

vulgar —common

want —to lack

weeds —clothing

what ho —"hello, there!"

wherefore —why

wit —intelligence; sanity

withal —moreover; nevertheless

without —outside

would —wish

 SHAKESPEARE EXPLAINED: MACBETH

Suggested Essay Topics

1. How would you characterize the relationship between Macbeth and Lady Macbeth? What do they have in common? What do they see differently? Do you think they love one another? Or is power more important than love?

2. One of the central concerns in *Macbeth* is the examination of gender roles. What does the play say about what it means to be a man and what it means to be a woman? In what ways have gender roles changed for men and women since Elizabethan times? In what ways haven't they changed?

3. What are your thoughts about the witches? What role do they play in *Macbeth*? Do you think they can control the future or just predict it? Is there a difference? Does Macbeth choose his future or is it already predetermined by fate?

4. We hear a lot today about leadership. How would you compare and contrast the leadership styles of Macbeth and Macduff? Are there any ways in which their styles are similar? How about ways in which they are different?

5. The two most prominent motifs in *Macbeth* are the symbols of darkness and blood. Choose one and show how Shakespeare uses it to contribute to our understanding of the play. Does the symbol you've chosen have any particular meaning for any of the characters in the play?

6. Why isn't this play called *Macduff*? Isn't he the real hero in *Macbeth*? Doesn't he represent good, and doesn't good overcome evil in the end?

7. If you could be any character in *Macbeth*, who would it be? How would you prepare for the part? What about the character would you emphasize in your performance?

Testing Your Memory

1. Which of the following lines does Macbeth *not* say? a) "[Life] is a tale told by an idiot, full of sound and fury,/Signifying nothing"; b) "Will all great Neptune's ocean wash this blood/Clean from my hand?"; c) "Unsex me here"; d) "Damned be him that first cries, 'Hold enough!'"

2. Who says the line above that Macbeth *doesn't* say? a) Banquo; b) Macduff; c) the Weird Sisters; d) Lady Macbeth.

3. Banquo's ghost attends the Macbeths' banquet because: a) he's hungry; b) he wants Macbeth to see the evil he's responsible for; c) he doesn't want to disappoint Lady Macbeth; d) he's waiting for his son's ghost to join him.

4. Which of the witches' prophecies *doesn't* come true? a) Macbeth becomes King of Scotland; b) Birnam Wood comes to Dusinane Hill; c) Macbeth's descendants become kings; d) Macbeth is killed by someone not of woman born.

5. Match each quotation below with the person who said it:
   a) Macbeth; b) Lady Macbeth; c) the Weird Sisters; d) Porter.
   1) "Thou shalt get kings though thou be none."
   2) "I have no spur to prick the sides of my intent, but only/Vaulting ambition."
   3) "Out damned spot!"
   4) "This place is too cold for hell."

6. Macduff is not "of woman born" because: a) he was hatched; b) his mother died during childbirth; c) he was delivered by means of a Caesarian section; d) men didn't believe in the equality of women.

7. How does Birnam Wood arrive at Dunsinane? a) as firewood for the winter; b) as camouflage for the English Army; c) as a coronation gift from Macduff; d) as wood used to make Macbeth's throne.

8. How does Lady Macbeth reportedly die? a) Her husband strangles her for nagging him; b) Macduff kills her for abandoning her husband; c) Malcolm poisons her for refusing to become his queen; d) She commits suicide.

9. On the night of Duncan's murder, Macbeth imagines he sees: a) a dagger floating in the air; b) Duncan's ghost saying he won't get away with his crime; c) Lady Macbeth packing her bags for England; d) his own death.

10. Which of the following *isn't* one of the witches' apparitions? a) an armed head that says, "Macbeth! beware Macduff"; b) a bloody child that says "none of woman born / Shall harm Macbeth"; c) a crowned child with a tree in his hands who tells Macbeth he'll never be vanquished until Birnam Wood comes to Dusinane; d) a halo to be worn by Macbeth after he dies and his soul enters heaven.

11. What does Lady Macbeth recommend for Macbeth to wash away the blood from his hands? a) lemon juice; b) ginger ale; c) water; d) none of the above.

12. Why does Macduff kill Macbeth? a) Macbeth has killed his wife and children; b) Macbeth has killed Duncan and Banquo; c) Macbeth has become a tyrant; d) All of the above.

13. What does Macbeth hope to gain by killing Duncan? a) a castle on Loch Ness; b) the crown of Scotland; c) peace of mind; d) revenge for the king's choosing Banquo as successor.

14. Who do the Macbeths blame for the murder of Duncan? a) Shakespeare; b) the drunken porter; c) Banquo and his son, Fleance; d) the sleeping chamberlains.

15. Which best describes Lady Macbeth the last time we see her? a) She's exhausted from burying all the people she murdered; b) She's gone mad with guilt from having helped murder Duncan;

c) She's angry with her husband's refusal to abdicate the throne;

d) She's furious with Macbeth for inviting Duncan to dinner.

16. What great lesson does Macduff teach Malcolm, the heir to the Scottish throne? a) Feeling deep pain and loss is not unmanly; b) Cutting taxes will keep the people loyal; c) There is no problem that can't be overcome by laughter; d) He has a lot to learn about women.

17. What's the weather like the night King Duncan is murdered? a) raining as usual; b) sunny, a sign of good things to come; c) unusually dark and stormy; d) foggy, perfect for going unseen at night.

18. Why does Fleance and not his father, Banquo, manage to escape from the murderers Macbeth has sent to kill them? a) Fleance is destined to be king; b) Fleance manages to stay on his horse; c) Banquo mistakes the murderers for monks; d) Fleance fights off his attackers.

19. When Macbeth says, "I dare do all that may become a man;/Who dares do more is none," he means: a) A man can do only so much work before he becomes an animal; b) To murder Duncan is to be a man no longer, but a monster; c) Ask me no questions and I'll tell you no lies; d) Once I kill Duncan and become king, I will no longer be ordinary.

20. When Lady Macbeth asks the spirits to "Come to my woman's breasts,/And take my milk for gall," she means: a) The milk in my breasts has turned to gall because I've never had children; b) Turn the milk in my breasts to gall so my child will take milk from his bottle; c) Take away from me everything female so I can murder like a man; d) Because my husband has the milk of human kindness flowing in his veins, the milk in my breasts has turned to gall.

Answer Key

Further Information

BOOKS

Macbeth (Folger Shakespeare Library). New York: Washington Square Press, 2003.

Macbeth (Shakespeare Graphic Library). New York: Black Dog and Leventhal, 2006.

Rosen, Michael, and Robert Ingpen. *Shakespeare: His Work and His World.* Cambridge, MA: Candlewick Press, 2006.

WEB SITES

Absolute Shakespeare is a resource for the Bard's plays, sonnets, and poems and includes summaries, quotes, films, trivia, and more. http://absoluteshakespeare.com

Shakespeare Online: Macbeth
  Text of the play, with resources including essays on diverse topics, for example, blood imagery, mysticism, and Hecate's role in the play. http://www.shakespeare-online.com/plays/macbethscenes.html

Play Shakespeare: The Ultimate Free Shakespeare Resource features all the play texts with an online glossary, reviews, a discussion forum, and links to festivals worldwide.
  http://www.playshakespeare.com

FILM

Macbeth. The Royal Shakespeare Company Production (1978) with Ian McKellen and Dame Judi Dench. Directed by Trevor Nunn.

AUDIO BOOK

Macbeth. The Caedmon Recording (1996) with Anthony Quayle and Stanley Holloway.

Bibliography

Bloom, Harold. *Shakespeare: The Invention of the Human.* New York: Riverhead Books, 1998.

———, ed. *Shakespeare's* Macbeth. New York: Chelsea House, 1987.

Bradley, A. C. *Shakespearean Tragedy: Lectures on Hamlet, Othello, King Lear and Macbeth.* New York: Palgrave Macmillan, 2007.

Bryson, Bill. *Shakespeare: The World as Stage.* New York: HarperCollins, 2007.

Harbage, Alfred. *William Shakespeare: A Reader's Guide.* New York: Octagon Books, 1971.

Hawkes, Terence, ed. *Twentieth-Century Interpretations of Macbeth: A Collection of Critical Essays.* Englewood Cliffs, NJ: Prentice-Hall, 1977.

Holland, Norman. *The Shakespearean Imagination.* New York: Macmillan, 1964.

Knight, G. Wilson. *The Wheel of Fire: Interpretations of Shakespearean Tragedy.* London: Routledge, 2001.

Muir, Kenneth. *Shakespeare's Tragic Sequence.* London: Routledge, 2005.

Shakespeare, William. *The Norton Shakespeare*, ed. Stephen Greenblatt. New York: W.W. Norton, 1977.

Siegel, Paul. *Shakespearean Tragedy and the Elizabethan Compromise.* New York: New York University Press, 1957.

Spurgeon, Caroline F. E. *Shakespeare's Imagery and What It Tells Us.* Cambridge, U.K.: Cambridge University Press, 1935.

Index

Page numbers in **boldface** are illustrations.

About the Author

Richard Andersen is a former Fulbright Professor of American Literature, James Thurber Writer in Residence, and Karolyi Foundation Fellow. His twenty-three books include six books on writing, five novels, five critical studies of well-known authors, a biography, and *Arranging Deck Chairs on the Titanic: Crises in Education*. *Getting Ahead*, a guide to successful career skills, has been translated into three languages. Springfield College, where Dr. Andersen teaches writing and literature, nominated him in 2003 for the Carnegie Foundation's United States Professor of the Year Award.